Tomorrow's England

Thaks for dinner

Best wishes

Nigel

Nigel Hastilow

Who would be free themselves must strike the blow - Byron

I will not be pushed, filed, stamped, indexed, briefed, debriefed or numbered. My life is my own. - Patrick McGoohan, "The Prisoner".

Published by
Halesowen Press
Church Chambers
High Street
Halesowen
B63 3BB

www.nigelhastilow.co.uk
www.halesowenpress.co.uk

Printed by
Vale Press Limited
Willersey
Worcestershire
WR12 7RR

Contents

For Fiona and Sheila

1
Tomorrow's people

It is August 2005. I receive a text message: "Was at the Cameron launch. It marks a new agenda that is exceptional, fluent, compassionate, progressive, pragmatic, young and sexy. It is without doubt the future of Conservatism. Am hugely buoyed. Davis is dull and pedestrian and doomed to electoral failure."

I reply: "It says here..."

He says: "Get your name as a supporter on his web-site."

I reply: "No point, he won't win."

He says: "Yes he will. Get on board, we're doomed with any of the others."

I reply: "It will be between DD (David Davis) and KFC (Ken Clarke)."

He says: "We're fxxxxx then."

Those text messages came at the launch of David Cameron's bid for the leadership of the Conservative Party, long before he wooed and won the members with his speech at the 2005 party conference. Cameron had only been in Parliament four years and was only 38. How, his critics asked, could he put up much of a challenge to Tony Blair or Gordon Brown? The Old Etonian PR man (adviser to Carlton TV) and ex-Tory party aide said we should all be more civilised, which is nice. He's my sister's MP and she likes him very much. She says he's got a very nice wife as well.

He stormed ahead of the front-runner David Davis, who was noted for his firm Paddy Ashdown jaw and his experience as a part-time member of the SAS. Trained to kill, his critics said he usually couldn't be bothered. Arrogance and laziness were allegedly his major disadvantages. Certainly he flopped badly at the party conference and never recovered.

He was one of those politicians who became the Next Big Thing having risen without a trace. Still, it's just as hard to believe, now, that there was every any serious thought given to the chances of Kenneth Clarke taking over as Tory leader. Clarke, known to all and sundry either as the most laddish Tory for many years or as an intransigent Europhile who couldn't be trusted not to sell out his country to the European Union – or both – came from a different era.

Ken – the great sport-watching, bird-watching, pint-drinking, jazz-loving cigar smoker – had various drawbacks including his age (65 – almost 70 by the time of the next election) and a lucrative job with a tobacco company being the most obvious.

There was speculation about his chances of appealing beyond the boundaries of the party. The voters liked his insouciance. He had lots of experience in top jobs including health, education and the Treasury.

There were also-rans such as Liam Fox, the former chairman of the party (I wrote to him once offering my services to the party for free but as he never bothered to reply he didn't get my vote). A doctor who can talk with authority about the NHS, his real claim to fame is being credited on the sleeve notes of ex-*Neighbours* star Natalie Imbruglia's first album. But he couldn't be leader because he's Scottish and it wouldn't do for every party leader to come from north of Hadrian's Wall.

That also ruled out Sir Malcolm Rifkind, the former Foreign Secretary, the MP for Kensington and Chelsea with the posh Miss Jean Brodie Edinburgh accent. Anyway, like several of his rivals, he was tainted with the disasters of the Major years.

As for the rest, it was a pretty feeble bunch. Theresa May, another ex-Chairman, best known for her allegedly sexy kitten heel shoes and for branding the Conservatives "the nasty party". Or Andrew Lansley, to which the only real response was: Who? The rank outsiders included Lord Seb Coe, once again a national hero after winning the 2012 Olympics for London and New Labour; ex-Big Brother housemate and gay Tory speechwriter Derek Laud; or William Hague. Ah, William Hague. Credible, available, able – William Hague would be welcomed back with open arms by the party and would be given a much better run by the voters and media now he's older and wiser than he was in 2001. But he refused to stand. Rumour and gossip insists the idea was ruled out by his wife, Ffion.

So we got to examine David Cameron at close quarters. And it became clear pretty quickly that he was not interested in appealing to those people who join the Conservative Party because it's full of crusty, old fashioned types who believe the country's gone to the dogs. For the Cameroons, nostalgia is yesterday's news. Those who believe our country's best days are behind us, who are pessimistic about the future, and consider "fings ain't wot they used to be", are history as far as DC is concerned.

Gradually the contenders dropped out of the running and it became clear Cameron would be voted in as leader of the Conservative Party by a landslide, leaving his rival David Davis and old-fashioned grumpy old men floundering in his wake. For Dave Cameron, bright star of the Conservative future, Margaret Thatcher was ancient history.

As he was happy to point out, tomorrow's voters weren't even born when she left office. It was meaningless for the party to hark back to past glories. Thatcherism, whatever it may have been, was as obsolete now as Marxism was in her day. Cameron's "modern, compassionate Conservatives" were a whole new breed, even if they were mainly educated at Eton and generally the offspring of the rich or the very rich. They were, however, untainted by the "nasty party" image of their predecessors, free of the baggage of union-bashing, spending cuts, lining the pockets of the rich, destroying public services etc. The Cameron Conservatives hate being described as "Tory lite", "Blairites in blue" or "Tone clones". But these Notting Hill trendies were picking up their party and plonking it down in the centre ground of British politics.

During the protracted leadership election campaign, and even though it was over almost before it began, the two candidates felt obliged to cross the country staging rallies. I went to see Dave in action at Millennium Point in Birmingham three days after seeing David at Warwick University. The contrasts were striking.

David was working class and emphasised his roots. He told his student audience he would never have been able to study at Warwick, where he took degree in molecular and computer science, if he'd been forced to pay tuition and top-up fees.

Dave (Eton and Oxford) said we just have to accept them.

David worked in industry and represented the grim-oop-north constituency of Haltemprice & Howden.

Dave had been a full-time, back-room politico since leaving university, except when he honed his PR skills working for Carlton TV. He represented the county set in Witney, Oxfordshire.

David had been an MP since 1987 and was 57; Dave had been in the Commons four years and he was 38. David had Ministerial experience; Dave had made three speeches as an Opposition front bench spokesman.

David had never taken any drugs; Dave wouldn't say but cleverly used the question to glean extra publicity for his campaign.

David blew his chances of becoming leader at the party conference; Dave flew.

At Warwick University, Mr Davis spoke without notes and demonstrated a strong grasp of policy issues – even esoteric questions such as the tax rate in Norway didn't faze him. He was passionate and caring. He spoke optimistically of the future. His event was run by a couple of young men. Two clever-clever students asked sarcastic questions. Afterwards, Mr

Davis stood in the rain waiting for a TV crew to ask a few desultory questions.

Mr Cameron's event was in the multi-million-pound Millennium Point, built with lottery money. It contains a modern museum called The Thinktank which, in turn, contains a Young People's Parliament. It was here he held his rally.

Young supporters gave speeches and we watched a video of the great man. He was then introduced by none other than Karren Brady, the boss of Birmingham City Football Club, the first lady of football. She was not, at that stage, a member of the Conservative Party but that didn't stop her telling us David Cameron had everything needed in a young and ambitious leader. How she could be so certain was not revealed.

Her insights into people are clearly more profound then most people's. They must be. She'd scarcely met Cameron before she was extolling his virtues to the Tory party and the world.

"We absolutely need enthusiasm – that wonderful ingredient you can't teach people – and we need that if we are going to take the party back to being fantastic," she declared. She said Mr Cameron had leadership qualities, ambition, determination, the right attitude, a sense of direction, he was positive and persistent. Ms Brady said his relative youth was a positive advantage. She took over at St Andrew's when she was 23 and had turned the loss-making club into a successful premiership team with a £45 million turnover and a £6 million profit. Little of this stands up to close scrutiny, especially as her boss, the millionaire pornographer David Sullivan, was at the same time complaining he was forced to pump more cash into the club to keep it afloat after it had been relegated to the First Division.

Anyway, it made a suitable introduction for the main attraction – Cameron himself. He walked in to a standing ovation, stood on the stage and spoke without notes, holding his hands before him in an attitude at once preacherly and humble. He answered questions and then used the Young People's Parliament's voting facilities to "ask the audience" what we thought about various issues. The answers, rather like the questions, were irrelevant.

He was thanked by Karren before departing to another standing ovation.

Mr Davis's do was rough and ready; Cameron's was a slick and smart. Davis looked like a competent Government Minister. He also looked like someone who knew he was going to lose. Cameron and his entire party knew he was going to win. Easily.

The Cameron effect is the most remarkable phenomenon in the post-Blair political world. His arrival immediately forced the Liberal Democrats to ditch their most successful leader for 80 years, replacing Charlie Kennedy with Sir Menzies Cambell. It was not a success.

More to the point, Cameron's arrival forced the Labour Party into genuine turmoil as backbenchers and, indeed, Ministers were, for the first time, forced to take seriously the risk that they might lose their seats. When the Labour Party realised what it was up against, some people thought there was a need to ditch Gordon Brown altogether and look for someone more voter-friendly to succeed Tony Blair and face Cameron's Conservatives.

Raising the possibility of Labour taking fright at the sight of a young Tory leader was, of course, proof of the potency of the new power in the Conservative Party. Cameron may be posh, he may be slick, he may be Tony's Tory doppelganger. But the man is the message. He was proof that the Conservatives had finally abandoned political dogma and endless in-fighting; that they'd had enough of being ignored or laughed at or despised.

Cameron's party fell in love with him overnight. More importantly, so did the media. All those middle-of-the-road hacks who churned out their newspaper columns at £4 a word were falling over each other to build up the new young hero. Newspapers want something new. Cameron became what Tony Blair once was – the young, thrusting, energetic face of the future.

But who is Cameron? What world is he giving us and how does it differ both from past Conservative worlds and from the New Labour world we have grown accustomed to? What is "compassionate Conservatism"? Does "vote blue, go green" mean anything? Is a new logo of a child's sketch of an oak tree the answer?

David Cameron is an Old Etonian. So are most of his closest supporters. He lives in the metropolitan and sophisticated Notting Hill area of London and so do most of his chums. He is very rich and so are most of his chums. He is married to the, albeit tattooed, arty and mildly rebellious, daughter of a landed Scottish baronet. He used to go riding in the Cotswolds. He represents an Oxfordshire constituency and ought to be a traditional huntin', shootin' and fishin' country boy who cares about the death of fox hunting and the destruction of the countryside.

That's certainly what the locals in Witney thought they were getting when they selected him to succeed the traitorous ex-Tory turncoat Shaun Woodward. It's probably what many true blue Tories thought they were voting for when they elected him as party leader. They were probably not listening to what he said, merely looking at his youth and charm and hoping for the best.

But of course Cameron claims to have been elected with a mandate to change his party, drag it into the 21st century etc. And every time he is attacked by the right-wingers in the Conservative Party, it's another piece of evidence to support the claim that he really is making a dramatic difference.

Whenever an old bruiser like Norman Tebbit complains and condemns, Cameron and his crew are delighted. It proves they are winning. The more such "friendly fire" the better for, in future, every time the old Thatcherite right-wing of the party launches a broadside they succeed only in proving Cameron's case for him.

The whole aim of the new leader was to re-model the Tories, to create a party the voters will actually warm to so when his own, unreconstructed right-wing head-bangers denounce his leadership, they play straight into Cameron's hands. "Look how far we have come and how fast," he can tell the uncommitted, the disillusioned Labour voters and the highly sheepish ex-Lib Dem supporters. "We've abandoned Thatcherism. Look – even Lord Tebbit says we have so it must be true."

When first Neil Kinnock and then Tony Blair tried to change the Labour Party, they demonstrated it by picking fights with their left-wingers. Lord Kinnock famously denounced the loony "Militant Tendency", provoked a party conference walkout by the Liverpudlian left and banned its members. Mr Blair picked a fight with the left by ripping up Clause Four of the party constitution, which went on about common ownership of the means of production, and winning a referendum of the rank and file. People like Tony Benn never forgave them but it was part of a necessary process aimed at proving the party was no longer red in tooth and claw, was sensible, moderate and competent and could be trusted to run the country again without destroying the economy, intro-ducing Socialism or taxing us out of existence.

David Cameron is doing the equal and opposite, picking very similar battles with his own extremists.

Immediately on taking over, he started to jettison much of what the party had fought for at a General Election which took place only a few months earlier; policies he had helped put in place and shape as a result of his role in helping to write the 2005 election manifesto.

Instead, he started to raise concerns which hardly registered as blips on the party's radar in the past, or registered only to be rejected, such as global warming, social inclusion and public services. Cameron is deadly serious about them all – to the point where he fought the 2006 local elections from an ice floe in the remote Norwegian island of Svalbard, urging people to "vote blue, go green". As for social inclusion, he takes every opportunity to visit inner city sink estates and projects to rescue the poor, unemployed and criminal. His "N. H. S." party conference speech in 2006 was an inspired marketing ploy, trying to re-brand the Tories as a party which uses and cares deeply about what is still the country's best-loved institution.

The compassionate Cameroon Conservatives don't want to talk about traditional right-wing issues like tax, immigration and the EU any more. They dropped plans for NHS "patients' passports", they support university top-up fees and don't want any more grammar schools. As for tax cuts, they want to "share the proceeds of growth" by giving more money to the public sector. And Cameron invented a most inspired piece of propaganda when he declared the party would not put tax cuts ahead of economic stability – as if, somehow, tax cuts were destabilizing to the economy instead of being central to its long-term growth and competitiveness.

It was all a bit of a shock for many Tories. As Lord Tebbit said, Cameron was moving his party onto the crowded centre ground where "he will finish in a dogfight with the Liberals and New Labour, all of whom would be saying things which were very similar to each other". The snag, according to Lord Tebbit, whose nicknames include the "Chingford strangler" and who was once described as "a semi house-trained polecat", is that Mr Cameron would alienate natural supporters. He would "leave a lot of people on the Right of politics – voters – feeling disenfranchised in the same way that Tony Blair has left a lot of people on the Left of politics feeling disenfranchised", according to Lord Tebbit.

It's a view which gained support among party members. A Conservative MP said that if Simon Hughes had won the Lib Dem leadership contest "New Labour will be run by a Tory, the Tories will be run by a Liberal and the Lib Dems will be run by a Socialist". Several Conservative MPs now take to addressing meeting of members by saying: "As you know I didn't vote for David Cameron but..." That way they distance themselves from the decisions while associating themselves with the subsequent rewards.

Conservative Party members knew when they elected Cameron they were voting for change. But for a party made up – by definition – of traditionalists resistant to change and keen to "conserve", the Cameron revolution has been as painful as the party's increasing popularity was pleasurable. Whenever two or three Conservatives are gathered together, dark mutterings can be heard about the direction of their party.

One of the few areas where Cameron, as a new leader, was able to practice what he preached was in the selection of candidates for Parliamentary constituencies. This was something even an impotent Leader of the Opposition could influence. Cameron and his loyal lieutenants, notably Francis Maude, at the time the party chairman, decided they needed tangible evidence that the party had changed. What better than to let the voters see for themselves by selecting more women and "BME" candidates? BME, by the way, is the latest politically-correct shorthand for people who are either black or from other ethnic minorities.

It was a policy whose time had come. Everywhere you look the only group to be reviled and rejected these days is the one which, in the past, was the most dominant of all: white, middle class, middle aged, heterosexual men like David Cameron are the most rejected, despised and unwanted.

This politically-correct policy has, in the past, been popular in some parts of the Labour Party. But not with the members or voters. Labour lost – and then lost again at a by-election – the ultra-safe seat of Blaenau Gwent, in Wales. Peter Law took the seat in 2005 in protest at the imposition of an all-women shortlist for the selection of the official Labour candidate. He romped home with a 9,121 majority in a seat once held by Aneurin Bevan and, later, by Michael Foot. When he died, a supporter, Dai Davis, beat the official Labour candidate in the Parliamentary by-election and his wife, Trish Law, took his seat in the Welsh Assembly.

Yet this was the policy adopted by David Cameron, Francis Maude and "Madonna's mother-in-law" Shireen Richie, film-maker Guy's mother and a leading light in the Westminster Conservative Party. The aim was to make the party more media-friendly at the BBC and similar organisations. As the BBC's ex-political editor, Andrew Marr, said of his employer: "The BBC is not impartial or neutral. It's a publicly funded, urban organisation with an abnormally large number of young people, ethnic minorities and gay people. It has a liberal bias not so much a party-political bias. It is better expressed as a cultural liberal bias." David Cameron's aim was to make the party acceptable to the BBC because otherwise it would never receive fair play with that broadcaster or the many fellow-travellers who take their cue from it. These include that phalanx of journalistic pundits who grub a living in the lucrative world between the Corporation and the printed word. They may not be directly employed by the BBC but they are inculcated with its "cultural liberal bias", they reinforce it and represent it. These people are, as the Conservatives recognised 15 years after Peter Mandelson had suborned anyone left to suborn, the "opinion formers" whose views somehow manage to insinuate themselves into the collective sub-conscious and become, for want of anything better, the received wisdom.

From the days of Margaret Thatcher until the dawn of David Cameron, the received wisdom was that the Conservatives were, as Theresa May so eloquently put it, "the nasty party". To reverse that trend, to become the nice party, the caring party, the – in another of Cameron's coinages – "caring Conservatives" it was necessary to jettison most of the baggage which got him into power. Hence the controversial A list of female and "BME" candidates, the refusal to let tax cuts come before economic stability, the campaign to "save the NHS" from Gordon Brown's cuts, the row over grammar schools in the summer of 2007, the new-found concern for the environment, and so on.

There are those – most of them members of the Conservative Party – who believe that when David Cameron comes to power, he will abandon his gloss of caring, sharing, co-operative conservatism and reveal himself to be the unreconstructed Thatcherite the Tory right would want him to be. Alas for those of a nostalgic disposition, David Cameron's changes had to be more than skin deep to have any meaning. Like Tony Blair before him, Cameron's job was not just to transform the image of his party but – as far as he could – to change its substance as well.

In the long run, Tony Blair failed. But Blair won three General Elections in a row before anybody noticed and before his own left wing decided they might as well rebel against their party's drift to the right now there was nothing left to lose. The same may one day happen to the Cameroon Conservatives. But if they win three elections before it all falls apart, nobody will complain except those left behind to pick up the pieces.

In the 1990s, Labour's left-wingers had a choice between backing Tony Blair to win power or sticking to their principles and staying lost in the political wilderness. They chose power. It is a not unreasonable decision because no matter how strong your principles, you can't do anything if you spend your political life on the outside trying to get in.

In exactly the same way, David Cameron knows very well that irritated right-wingers have nowhere else to go and will probably continue to vote Conservative come what may. Lord Tebbit and like-minded traditionalists know a centrist, moderate Conservative Party which wins elections is better than a right-wing, reactionary one which sticks to its Thatcherite principles and keeps on losing.

As Karl Marx said: "There's no change without sacrifice." Especially when many people would see the abandonment of Thatcherism as no sacrifice at all. Even those who look back with nostalgia to the past are willing to embrace the future with David Cameron. As one member of his Shadow Cabinet told me: "Half a Conservative Government is better than no Conservative Government at all."

2

Welcome to tomorrow

What sort of a country would Prime Minister David Cameron inherit? What sort of legacy did Tony Blair hand on to Gordon Brown – bearing in mind that the latter was as responsible as his former friend for the state we're in?

It will be a nation in turmoil. A police state. A country with an identity crisis.

In spite of the attention devoted to Cameron and Gordon Brown, if we are not careful, their comings and goings may well count for less and less as the huge super-state of the European Union expands its borders still further, importing immigration and terrorism at the same time. The EU will not relinquish any of its existing powers and, in tomorrow's England, it will continue to expand its power in spite of the peoples of Europe, some of whom have voted against just such an agglomeration in a referendum.

In tomorrow's England the health service may well collapse; we will be more scared than ever to express our opinions freely or make a joke; families will pretty much be things of the past.

In tomorrow's England, the many faiths and languages expressed in our towns and cities will continue to multiply. It is likely England will remain under continual threat from terrorists, home-grown and imported. We will be told this has nothing to do with race or religion and ordered, on pain of criminal sanctions, to remain tolerant. Even in the face of separatism and deliberately-chosen ghettos.

Our concern for security has become increasingly fraught. It may well become worse as new outrages are perpetrated. Then we may wake up one morning to discover our freedoms have disappeared. Traditional

Magna Carta rights such as freedom of speech, the right of assembly and the right to trial by jury could all be snatched from us in the wake of a terrorist attack. We won't even mind – at the time. And when we wonder if we should object, it will be too late. Again.

In tomorrow's England, we will have no choice but to accept constant, 24-hour, scrutiny of all our activities. Someone, somewhere, will know everything about you: how you spend your money and what you like to buy, what web-sites you visit and where you walk, where you drive, how fast and in what car, when you go abroad and when you catch a tube. And that's without being forced to carry an identity card.

In tomorrow's England, you will be expected to travel by bus, face a hefty penalty for using a car, or you will have to stay at home. You will be persecuted for owning a four-by-four off-road vehicle, for putting your rubbish into the wrong bin and for flying abroad on holiday. You will be pilloried for destroying the planet if you do not shiver in the winter, block up your fireplace, throw away your patio heater and stick within your allocated carbon footprint.

The green fields of tomorrow's England will be concreted over to accommodate the ten or eleven million extra people who will be living here by the year 2050.

In tomorrow's England, we may finally tire of the Scots and grant them their wish of independence. This would, of course, embarrass Gordon Brown and cause consternation in the Labour Party which relies on Scotland to maintain its power over England.

In tomorrow's England, the electoral system will continue to be abused as if we were living in a banana republic.

Welcome to tomorrow.

3
Lunch-time for losers

Lunch-time in the bank queue at Barclays in Birmingham's New Street. The number of assistants halves as the number of customers doubles, so there's plenty of time to listen to the gossip that goes on around you. Immediately behind me two young women are discussing mobile phones and boyfriends. They chatter away in their Brummie accents quite happily as we all wait for someone willing to give us back some of our own money.

As they gossip away they sound exactly like all the other teenagers you ever listen to. I turn towards the door wondering whether it's worth waiting any longer or whether I can remember my PIN number. I see the girls for the first time. And I have to confess, though I know I shouldn't be, that I am shocked. Because these two girls, who must be teenagers and who have all the phrases, likes and dislikes of teenagers, are none-theless clad from head to toe in black, except for small slits for their eyes.

They are Moslem women hidden behind the veil of their faith. According to Polly Toynbee in the "Guardian", "the top-to-toe burka, with its sinister, airless little grille, is more than an instrument of persecution, it is a public tarring and feathering of female sexuality. It transforms any woman into an object of defilement too untouchably disgusting to be seen".

I'm not sure she's right. Former Foreign Secretary Jack Straw provoked a national debate on the issue after saying he asked Moslem women who came to see him in his Blackburn constituency to lift their veils when they talked to him. He liked to see their faces because expression is part of communication. The argument raged to and fro for days with some people siding with the Toynbee line that it represents the suppression of women and others who argued the decision to take the veil in this way actually represents an act of defiance, if not aggression, on the part of the wearer, demonstrating her opposition to, and alienation from, the Western world in which she lives. There was even an infamous photograph of a group of veiled Moslem women in Birmingham taken as one of them gave a very defiant V-sign to the snapper – a symbol, perhaps, of the real attitude of those behind the veil in England today.

It has to be said the two young women in the queue at Barclays Bank in Birmingham seem perfectly normal, happy wearers of this garb. They may have been forced to go out in the burka by their repressive men-folk but there was no evidence to support this view.

Yet the sight of these girls is strange and mildly disturbing. Most of us can't understand why anyone would want to wear the burka.

The conversation of these two girls in the queue – boys, school and mobile phones – was modern, up-to-date and Western. In stark contrast, their clothes were positively medieval, antiquated and Middle Eastern. The girls embodied at that moment the dilemma facing so many Moslems in England and so many of the rest of us when we contemplate their co-religionists. We live in a secular, materialistic, predominantly Godless society yet many Moslems in this country take their faith much more seriously than the rest of us can reasonably imagine.

Which raises a serious and difficult question: To what extent should our tolerant, liberal, pluralistic society accommodate views which the majority of us find abhorrent and which, in some instances, seek to undermine the principles we live by? The rantings of the mad mullahs were, until the London underground suicide bombings, or 7/7 as they are now known, tolerated in the name of free speech, even though the law had some time earlier made it illegal to spit out the equal but opposite vitriol of the rabid right.

Since 9/11 and 7/7 we have become less tolerant of those who make themselves "the enemy within" but while we fight to preserve our tolerant liberalism, some commentators perform a bizarre form of self-abasement. They say how offensive our modern society is. They say they can understand why disaffected adolescent Muslim males might want to turn themselves into suicide bombers. These critics claim we are living in a world of sleaze, consumerism and atheistic hedonism which has no culture or values and is therefore worthy of the hate directed at it by the Al Qaeda network and its fellow travellers.

Yet we are lucky to live in the most successful, peaceful and harmonious society in the history of this country. It is not perfect but it is infinitely better than a repressive Taliban regime in Afghanistan or a dictatorship in Iraq.

It is not without its beliefs either. We all "believe in" democracy, the rule of law, tolerance, freedom of speech, freedom of association and freedom of worship. We all relish the benefits of capitalism. We are healthier, wealthier and wiser than we have ever been. Western society is not the peak of human perfection – just the best sort of society humanity has yet managed to invent or devise. While there are many, many things wrong with it, it is still an improvement on everything that's gone before.

We must not allow fanatical enemies of our world to mislead us into such self-loathing that we come to accept their account of society. We do not live in some kind of moral vacuum where decadence is eating away at the foundations of our world. People with strong religious beliefs are not in any way justified in throwing their lives away trying to destroy us.

We know this is the ambition of a few fanatical Moslems. They can accuse us of degeneracy and use their whipped-up moral indignation to justify their murderous actions.

The truth is that they are lucky to live in a world which respects all faiths, all creeds and all colours. If they don't realise it, that's their failure. Not ours. The youths who plot the downfall of 21st century Western society are not fired by faith and fervour. They are socially inadequate. They are failures. They don't know how lucky they are.

In the words of the veiled girls in the bank queue, they're losers.

Yet we are changing the face of England to accommodate these fanatics. We are giving up freedoms we have believed in and cherished for centuries. We are creating a brave new world which owes more to George Orwell than we may want to admit. This is taking place incrementally, stage by stage, step by step. It is doubtful if there is some sinister "Big Brother" who is the brains behind an evil plot – unfortunately every step along the primrose path to our self-incarceration is justifiable as a necessary method of protecting us from our unseen enemies.

And because there have been, and will be again, serious terrorist outrages in England and, indeed, throughout the world, we accept the need to limit and confine ourselves. We don't mind queuing for aeroplanes and having our nail scissors confiscated. We don't even notice the absence of litter bins at railway stations. We are not in the least concerned to see police officers toting sub-machine guns at road junctions. We say how pleased we are to feel protected.

We aren't even particularly concerned when we are banned from saying certain things or telling some jokes. We scarcely bat an eyelid when private organisations hold vast databases with information about every single financial transaction we have made in our adult lives. We are supremely indifferent to the possibility that our every move is monitored on all-pervasive surveillance systems. We don't mind much if the police shoot dead a terrorist suspect on the London Underground - even when it turns out they got the wrong man.

This is the kind of England we can expect to live in tomorrow and the day after tomorrow.

A couple of years ago I wrote "The Last of England" which described the slow death of our national identity and attributed its disappearance to a range of causes, including the Scottish Raj which has run our country since 1997; the triumph of the New Establishment of 1960s flower-power Socialists who came to their positions of power and influence around the time Tony Blair became Prime Minister; but also to inexorable historical processes, the rapid growth in the country's population, the decline in education standards and so on.

Most of what we once had as a country has now gone. Yet some of what remains is very precious indeed and should be preserved. Freedom is not an absolute. It is divisible. It can be eroded and abandoned and given up voluntarily. Man is born free but is everywhere in chains.

How far are we prepared to go in giving up our freedom? It looks as if we are prepared to go a very long way indeed. It looks as if we will bequeath to subsequent generations a country which is ruled and regulated to such an extent that the very concept of personal freedom will be an alien idea.

Of course, nominally we will all be free to do as we like. But there will always be someone watching us. Watching over us, you might say, in a benign and fatherly way. But it still amounts to checking every step we take, every move we make.

Everything we think, everywhere we go, every word we say, every pound we spend, our entire existence will be logged on databases. If we have nothing to hide, it is always said, we have nothing to fear.

But is that true?

4
I am not a number, I am a free man

In the 1967 TV series "The Prisoner", Patrick McGoohan ran around Portmeirion in North Wales being chased by bouncing balls and shouting: "I am not a number, I am a free man." He was actually Number Six. He never did get to find the answer to his perennial question: "Who is number one?"

It was a little like watching a paranoid failing to enjoy a lovely sunshine holiday at somewhere exclusive and exotic like Guantanamo Bay. The Prisoner was a number – and so are we all. If you want to buy anything now you must key in your PIN – your personal identification number. It's only four digits and yours may well be the same as mine – but we are now numbers, not people. To make matters worse, every credit and debit card we possess has its own number. So we could be a random series of maybe 13 digits rather than just the four.

As the Prisoner realises early on in the series, there's always someone looking at you. We are on CCTV wherever we go. The spy (safety) cameras aimed at milking motorists of money record where we are, where we're going and how fast we're travelling.

There are multi-million pound companies which own data about all of us. Every time we apply for a credit card, buy a TV from Curry's or log on to Amazon – whenever we transact any business – our activities are recorded and tracked. The details are then sold on either so we can be flogged "platinum" credit cards or so that we can be denied any loans in the future (or both, given that these systems are far from foolproof).

Meanwhile the Government and the EU are planning to extend the electronic tagging system being used at the moment simply to keep a few thugs and burglars out of our jails. Within five years they will be ready to install electronic tagging in every car in Britain to track where we go and charge us a new toll per mile. The EU's Galileo programme will see 30 satellites launched into space by 2010 with the main aim of spying on us all. One report says: "Freight systems have to be in place by 2009 with cars being in place by 2011."

The RAC will be delighted. The once-venerable Royal Automobile Club, which was so embarrassed by its Royal appellation it dropped the crown from its logo for being too old-fashioned, apparently thinks motorists should be persecuted even more than they are already.

"More effective deterrents do need serious and urgent consideration," according to the organisation, which wants immediate 12-month bans and electronic tagging of our cars even though the nationwide clamp-down on speeding has nothing whatsoever to do with road safety. The RAC may like to think it's campaigning to cut death and injuries on the roads but the reality is different.

The speed cameras on virtually every street are there to make money. About 6,000 cameras have been installed around the country in the past decade and, in just one year, motorists paid fines totalling £112 million. In the year 2003-4, about 1.8 million £60 fixed penalty notices were issued compared with 260,000 three years earlier. And the costs don't stop at a £60 fine, of course. The three point endorsement of our licences is worse, much worse.

The endorsements add up incredibly quickly and it can only be a matter of weeks or months – or maybe only a single journey – before you accumulate enough points to lose your licence. That, in turn, can mean losing your job, your home and quite possibly your marriage as well. A driving ban can destroy a motorist's life. All the more reason, I hear you say, for the motorist to stick to the speed limit. True, but all the more reason for the law to be fair, reasonable and proportionate. At the moment, attacks on speeding drivers are excessive, unfair and unreasonable. Especially when it's obvious the entire campaign is about raising money, not about road safety.

Obviously the usual shroud-waving road safety campaigners will claim otherwise. But if the Government, the police and local authorities were genuinely interested only in cutting down on death and injury, they wouldn't care if their speeding fine revenues were no longer rising. But they do care. Income from fines is substantial but as we get wise to the location of static speed cameras, that tax isn't rising as fast as it used to. So what do they do? Call up more mobile speed cameras which lie in wait to trap more drivers, not to protect road-users from harm.

It's worth adding that, of course, this is one of the many areas where you will be penalised if you try to abide by the law. Virtuous, properly taxed and insured motorists, are sure to be tracked down and prosecuted. There are more than two million people driving on our roads without licences, insurance, tax or any of the other documents needed to remain within the law. These people are not pursued over parking fines or speeding tickets. Indeed, generally they get detected only when it's too late and they have killed someone else (or possibly themselves). It is too expensive and too time-consuming for the police to chase up these people, even though they invariably drive the least roadworthy cars and are the most likely to drive dangerously. It's tempting to conclude that we would all be wiser avoiding our legal obligations altogether, safe in the knowledge than maybe only one in ten of us would ever be caught. But unfortunately the majority of us are simply too law-abiding, so we allow the tax-gatherers to treat us with contempt.

Speed cameras are one form of intrusion which, in some cases, is destroying people's lives. Yet we pretend it's all for the best and never mind the intrusion or surveillance.

When my niece opened her birthday cards on her 18th birthday there was one from her local Conservative MP, John Maples. Initially she was delighted. She thought I may have had something to do with it because I know him vaguely and I am active in the Conservative Party. Of course I had to deny any responsibility. She then wanted to know how Mr Maples knew it was her 18th birthday. I had to explain a computer would have alerted him to the fact that her name was on the electoral register and that she would be eligible to vote from that day onwards. Her reaction was that this was another example of how "they" are always spying on you. I couldn't disagree.

After all, if you can't shop without being noticed, you can't walk down a High Street without being filmed and you can't drive anywhere without being charged, it's no big deal if you aren't allowed out of the house without carrying your expensive identity card. The extent to which our freedoms have been compromised beggars belief.

When they filmed "The Prisoner" in the 1960s, they may have had a premonition of the kind of world we would inherit. But it was still the stuff of thrillers and fantasy. Today it's mundane, dull reality. It's commonplace. If we want to survive and enjoy life in the 21st century, we must be willing to abandon silly little notions like personal freedom. Because, after all, it is being sacrificed for the greater good.

To cut down on road congestion; to stop credit card fraud; to prevent social security fiddles; above all to clamp down on terrorists. What is there to complain about? If you've done nothing wrong, you have nothing to hide. If you have nothing to hide, you have nothing to fear.

In George Orwell's book "1984", the State – Big Brother – goes even further and polices what people think. "Thoughtcrime" is a serious offence. If you are guilty of thinking the wrong thoughts you are re-educated by the State until you become a good, submissive little citizen willing to fit in with the way things are. The book's hero Winston Smith is taken to Room 101 to face his worst fears and be purged of his politically incorrect ideas.

We, too, have an offence of "Thoughtcrime". You must work out for yourself what sorts of offences might fall under that heading because if I were to spell it out I might be arrested and prosecuted. The good news for "1984's" Winston Smith and "The Prisoner's" Number Six is that at least both our oppressed heroes were allowed to smoke a consoling cigarette. Even that is denied us now.

Why do we tolerate the Big Brother society when it plainly does not work – and certainly not in the citizen's best interests?

Take CCTV, for instance. It is supposed to prevent crime and help police detect criminals. But does it? From time to time, when a desperate police force announces another knife amnesty, they are likely to provide the local television station with CCTV videos of a terrible attack taking place in some town centre on a Friday night. We see grainy footage of yobs swaggering down a street and of innocent bystanders hanging around waiting for a bus. Then we see the yobs set upon the bystanders, kicking and punching them, before a knife is slipped between someone's ribs, or down his back, or across his face. Then we see the yobs swagger off again while the victim is dying in a pool of blood and his friend is incapable of standing. All this brought to our prime-time television screens courtesy of crime-preventing, criminal-detecting CCTV.

The cameras are everywhere. They track our innocent movements and trace our comings and goings all day and all night. Presumably someone, somewhere, is supposed to watch these dull broadcasts all day long as we drop into Beattie's or Superdrug, check out the window of M&S or the latest offers in the travel agent's window. All very, very dull.

So what happens when a couple of drugged-up, drunken louts lay about some innocent passers-by? Is the chap who patrols the CCTV camera screens alert and ready to press the alarm? Do the police respond instantaneously to the call? Is the crime prevented? Are the perpetrators apprehended? We all know the answers. No, the alarm is not raised. No, the police are not poised to leap into action. No, the crime is not prevented. No, the thugs are not caught.

What we have instead is useful footage to give to the TV stations to promote whatever latest wheeze the police PR people come up with in place of a policy of preventing and detecting crime. An example of how it works occurred to a young lad I know was walking home from the pub with a fellow student.

Some yobs called them gay and started to attack them. My young friend was left with knife wounds across his forehead and nose, on one arm and all down his back. His friend was so badly kicked he suffered eye injuries. At the age of 19, he has been told he can never again play rugby for fear of going blind.

This didn't happen in some seedy inner city. Or even straight after chucking-out time in some big metropolis. It took place in the quaint old county town of Shrewsbury. Just another Saturday night in England.

Were the police visible? Did they rush to rescue my young friend and his mate? Did they pounce on the scum who did this? No, of course not. But luckily they might possibly have CCTV to nail them. The local council web-site boasts: "One of the main tools in the fight against crime is the Shrewsbury Town Centre CCTV. A network of 27 colour, fully controllable cameras monitor public areas in Shrewsbury 24 hours a day, every day. With direct links to the Police and Town Centre Security Staff. CCTV operatives have been instrumental in helping reduce crime in Shrewsbury Town Centre."

To which the only proper response is: Big deal.

Still, if CCTV could not prevent the terrible attack, at least it might help catch the criminals. As luck would have it – luck is the operative word, I'm afraid, because the chances of it being the result of good detective work are modest indeed – as luck would have it, the police picked up the youths allegedly responsible for this frightening attack.
The police even tested their clothes and found plenty of the victims' blood on it. So far, so open and shut case. Unfortunately the youths claimed the blood only came to be on their clothes because they had rushed to the assistance of the victims and tried to look after them.

You might consider it surprising, then, that they were not tending to these wounds when the police arrived. Unfortunately the two victims can't identify their assailants. It was dark night and they were pounced on from behind.

So what about Shrewsbury's much-vaunted CCTV security system? It was of absolutely no help. But happily a young woman saw the attack. She had screamed at the thugs to stop. She was still there when the police and ambulance arrived, tending to the two victims. She even wanted to go to the hospital with the boys.

But she's a mystery girl. The boys, understandably, given the state they were in, didn't ask for her name and address and they'd never seen her before. The police, who might be expected to have a little more presence of mind, also didn't ask her who she was. She was the only independent witness to the attack – and the police failed even to ask for her name. They never found her again even though she was the only person who could possibly identify the assailants. She could refute the yobs' explanations of how their victims' blood got onto their clothes.

So when word came back from the Director of Public Prosecutions that there wasn't enough evidence to charge the yobs, the police expressed their sorrow and regret to the families of the victims. But there was nothing more they could do. As a result, somewhere in the Shrewsbury area is a gang of yobs which carried out a sickening attack on a couple of young men and got away with it.

Not long after this terrible incident, two prostitutes were murdered in a brothel in Shrewsbury. CCTV was of no help in identifying the killer. It is impossible to escape the conclusion that is it no deterrent. But where are the police when we need them? Hiding behind CCTV. Pretending that "27 fully controllable colour cameras" will somehow make the mean streets of Shrewsbury safe for innocent people.

In the small town where I used to live, the chavs laugh at the local community support officer and from time to time knock him off his bicycle. And they get away with it. These chavs cause more and more problems. They gather in the same place day after day, play football in the street, urinate inside the church, smash windows and fences. The good news is, though, that the police have come up with a wonderful solution to deal with this growing, low-level menace. They are assisting the locals in their campaign to get CCTV installed.

5
Every step you take...

As if the 4.2 million CCTV cameras costing taxpayers £500 million around the country, viewing us an average of 300 times a day, weren't bad enough, what about all the other ways our lives are monitored? As the Government's own Information Commissioner, Richard Thomas, warns we are "sleepwalking into a surveillance society". He says the people of Britain are under greater surveillance than anyone else in the industrialised world.

New ways of keeping tabs on us are being invented all the time. "Dataveillance" is the black art of combining information about the use of credit cards, mobile phones and loyalty cards to gather information on our buying habits. This is why most of us are subjected to so much marketing junk by e-mail, post and telephone. That's bad enough but what if the information is used, perhaps, to blackmail us? It might be argued that if we have nothing to hide, we have nothing to fear. But is that a good enough argument for such a massive and prolonged intrusion into the privacy of our lives? As Mr Thomas says: "We've got to say where do we want the lines to be drawn? How much do we want to have surveillance changing the nature of society in a democratic nation?"

There are cameras clocking car registration numbers. Originally they were aimed at tracking IRA terrorists. Now they're used to catch anyone who speeds or fails to pay a congestion charge.

Soon, every item in a shop will carry an ID tag of its own. This will not be removed when you buy it and take it home. They are similar to the tags some councils already put in people's refuse sacks to check whether they are throwing away the right rubbish. This has already led to people being fined for placing the wrong kind of rubbish in the wrong sack.

When the pop group The Police sang "every step you take, every move you make, I'll be watching you" there were two interpretations of the lyrics. The benign view was that this was a love song in which the lover was promising to watch over his loved one, to protect and care for her. The more sinister explanation, and the one that a moment's reflection would confirm as the more appropriate, is that this is a song by a stalker or psychopath threatening never to leave the object of his obsession alone for a moment.

This is a frightening threat. The stalker will be there all the time, looking, watching, waiting. At every street corner. In ever bar or shop. Even in the privacy of your home and bedroom. "I'll be watching you…."

There are laws against this. Stalkers are treated very seriously, even if they never go beyond following a few steps behind the object of their attentions down a crowded street. They are nightmarish figures, especially for women. Potentially dangerous. Occasionally murderous.

That's why the police take complaints about stalkers seriously. It's why they make great TV dramas. It's why we get a frisson of fear, a chill down the spine, when the subject comes under discussion.

So perhaps that is why we instinctively recoil from the idea that the State – Big Brother – is watching us all the time. Yet in the future, the intrusive society will get even worse than it is now.

The mother of all intrusions into our lives is the planned imposition of an Identity Card. We won't have to carry one. It will just become impossible for anyone but a complete recluse to avoid it.

Despite reports to that it will cost a fortune and won't prevent crime, terrorism or even identity theft, we will soon be forced to pay about £100 each for the privilege of carrying at all times an Identity Card. The Government claims this will be voluntary. The House of Commons Home Affairs Committee said: "To describe the first phase of the Government's proposals as voluntary stretches the English language to breaking point." These cards will have fingerprints and iris scans. We could be fined £2,500 if we refuse to submit and up to £1,000 if we need a replacement or if we forget to tell "them" that we have moved house.

If we find someone else's card and don't hand it in immediately, we could be jailed for up to two years.

It may be argued that we already have to show up to three forms of identification for even the simplest transaction these days so it will be much more convenient if we simply use one, universally-recognised *passe-partout*. Many people will adopt an ID card because it will be convenient. What they will disregard, perhaps until it's too late, is the fact that carrying the card will become compulsory; that walking down the road to the shop to buy a newspaper without an ID card on your person could become a criminal offence. There is no greater threat to personal freedom.

Yet we will sleepwalk into the adoption of ID cards because successive Home Office Ministers believe it will help to protect their jobs when the next terrorist outrage takes place. "At least he had an ID card," they will be able to say, as if the possession of such a piece of plastic somehow implies the Government had done everything it could to protect us. The terrorists responsible for the Madrid bombings in 2004 did have identity cards. It didn't stop them murdering 190 people.

As time goes by and computers become more capable of storing and accessing the information Ministers think they may one day need, the Government will – probably by accident rather than design – have created a national database with everything anyone would ever wish to know about each of us – all of it accessible through our ID cards. Name, age, weight, medical history, marital status, address, occupation, dependents, scars or personal identification, tax history, National Insurance status, eligibility and receipt of benefits, sexual orientation, colour, medical history....

This kind of information could be used for our benefit. It could also work against us because we can be absolutely positive the computer system will not work properly. It will record the wrong information. It will mix up one person with another. It will not be kept up to date. It simply won't work yet every official pronouncement will be that it is functioning perfectly. We will be at the mercy of a massive – massively flawed – database.

It's like the true story of the little girl who told her classmates at school one day: "My daddy bonked me last night." Daddy was arrested, locked up, quizzed, investigated and given an extremely hard time. Eventually the police accepted that in this context the word "bonked" referred to his having hit his daughter lightly over the head with a blow-up hammer. Nothing could have been more innocent. Daddy was exonerated. Let off without a stain on his character. Free to go. Five years later, he was rejected for a job. Because this incident has led to his name being included on a sex offenders register and nobody ever removed it again even though he had never committed any crime.

That's just one small example. The risks of intrusion, mistake and malice are almost infinite. Yet ID cards will allegedly save us from terrorism, reduce benefit fraud and make our lives easier.

The cards may contain fingerprints, iris scans or – though it's not admitted yet – DNA readings as well. That doesn't mean they won't be forged. The experience on the internet shows that no matter how sophis- ticated the security introduced into systems becomes, there are people who, for money, or just for the sake of the challenge, are able to circumvent them and cause immense damage. If a geek can crack the NASA computers he can crack a UK Identity Card system – not only forging new ones but, even more dangerously, obtaining access to the national database itself. No-one will be safe from the power of the State – or of the criminal.

One reasonable description of the way the ID card will work in conjunc- tion with the National Identity Register (NIR) – the massive central computer with all the records on it – was described in a widely circulated e-mail written by Frances Stonor Saunders, the former arts editor of The New Statesman, author of *The Cultural Cold War*, *Diabolical English- man* and *The Devil's Broker*. She says:

Every place that sells alcohol or cigarettes, every post office, every pharmacy, and every Bank will have an NIR Card Terminal, (very much like the Chip and Pin Readers that are everywhere now) into which your card can be 'swiped' to check your identity. Each time this happens, a record is made at the NIR of the time and place that the Card was presented. This means for example, that there will be a government record of every time you withdraw more than £99 at your branch of NatWest, who now demand ID for these transactions. Every time you have to prove that you are over 18, your card will be swiped, and a record made at the NIR. Restaurants and off licenses will demand that your card is swiped so that each receipt shows that they sold alcohol to someone over 18, and that this was proved by the access to the NIR, indemnifying them from prosecution.

Private businesses are going to be given access to the NIR Database. If you want to apply for a job, you will have to present your card for a swipe. If you want to apply for a London Underground Oyster Card, or a supermarket loyalty card, or a driving licence, you will have to present your ID Card for a swipe. The same goes for getting a telephone line or a mobile phone or an internet account.

Oyster, DVLA, BT and Nectar (for example) all run very detailed databases of their own. They will be allowed access to the NIR, just as every other business will be. This means that each of these entities will be able to store your unique number in their database, and place all your travel, phone records, driving activities and detailed shopping habits under your unique NIR number. These databases, which can easily fit on a storage device the size of your hand, will be sold to third parties either legally or illegally. It will then be possible for a non-governmental entity to create a detailed dossier of all your activities. Certainly, the government will have clandestine access to all of them, meaning that they will have a complete record of all your movements, from how much and when you withdraw from your bank account to what medications you are taking, down to the level of what sort of bread you eat - all accessible via a single unique number in a central database.

The Government is going to COMPEL you to enter your details into the NIR and to carry this card. If you and your children want to obtain or renew your passports, you will be forced to have your fingerprints taken and your eyes scanned for the NIR, and an ID Card will be issued to you whether you want one or not. If you refuse to be fingerprinted and eye scanned, you will not be able to get a passport. Your ID Card will, just like your passport, not be your property. The Home Secretary will have the right to revoke or suspend your ID at any time, meaning that you will not be able to withdraw money from your Bank Account, for example, or do anything that requires you to present your government issued ID Card.

The arguments that have been put forward in favour of ID Cards can be easily disproved. ID Cards WILL NOT stop terrorists; every Spaniard has a compulsory ID Card as did the Madrid Bombers. ID Cards will not 'eliminate benefit fraud', which in comparison, is small compared to the astronomical cost of this proposal, which will be measured in billions according to the LSE (London School of Economics). This scheme exists solely to exert total surveillance and control over the ordinary free British Citizen, and it will line the pockets of the companies that will create the computer systems at the expense of your freedom, privacy and money.

Unfortunately, despite the obvious destruction of freedom the ID card represents, when our civil liberties have been completely abandoned and we're all banned from leaving home without our card, companies like Excel Airways will have to take some of the blame.

Every test of public opinion shows that young people are the group most in favour of ID cards, because they need them most, mainly to get into pubs but also to obtain mobile phones and other necessities of life. At the moment they use (and lose) their passports. The snag is these flimsy documents wear out very quickly which is why Excel Airways banned my niece from flying on one of their 'planes because her passport was too dog-eared. Though the number of supporters of ID cards is dwindling, it's fine with the young.

Then there is the surveillance of our every financial transaction. When a young friend was refused a mobile phone credit agreement we took the trouble to ask why the credit rating of an 18-year-old with no financial history of any description was so bad he should be summarily refused credit. This elicited a response from a credit rating agency which had tied his creditworthiness to that of his father. We were sent through the post, without any concern for his father's privacy, a long list of his debts and various county court judgments outstanding against him. The details of his private financial affairs had been made public to us because not only had his son been branded a credit risk, though guilt by association, but so had my wife and I because our address was the young man's temporary home address and he was related to someone with a dubious financial history.

So, entirely without our knowledge, we had all been tarred with the same brush. Quite wrongly and unfairly. At the same time, details of the father's financial affairs had been given to us for the cost of a £5 administration fee without any questions asked. This invasion of privacy is taking place on a massive scale every day throughout the country.

One of these enormous private sector spy agencies is Experian. Their web-site warns: "Late payment, fraud or a clerical error can easily damage your credit status and lead to lenders refusing you credit. CreditExpert helps you to manage what's on your credit report and could save you money when you apply for a loan, mortgage or credit card. Join over 14 million people worldwide who have viewed their free online Experian credit report to better understand and manage their credit status."

The aim of this is to frighten you into paying £5.99 a month to be told what's happening to your credit rating. It's not surprising to discover that Experian has more than 12,500 staff in 32 countries and annual sales of over £1.7 billion. Spying on us is big business.

The company is big on identity theft – the process by which a crook assumes your identity or mine. That's because it's a booming business, it's pretty easy to achieve and it costs credit card companies, banks and other lenders a fortune when the crook uses our credit card to purchase goods in our name. That's why they imposed chip-and-pin technology on us, so that in theory only the card holder would know the right four-digit code and therefore fraud would fall (it did, by five per cent, though many criminals reverted to more tried-and-tested, old-fashioned methods of getting money and went back to armed robbery).

When I tried to pay for my new car tyres with a credit card, payment was refused. The tyre fitters were told to call Barclaycard; I was summoned to the phone. Had I bought £3,500-worth of furniture in Wolverhampton recently? I had not. Barclaycard were excellent. They cancelled my card and issued me with a new one. It didn't cost me a penny. I have no idea whether the people using my card were arrested or not. Nor do I know how they were able to pretend to be me in the first place. But I do know I came off lightly compared with some victims of identity theft, whose lives are left in limbo for weeks at a time.

As one of them said: "I cannot lease a car, buy a house or apply for a credit card. My life has been taken over by another."

I know someone who – thanks to a misunderstanding with her bank – was mistaken for an identity thief. As a result she was denied access to her own money for six weeks. It was a nightmare. At its worst, people take over your identity completely. To officialdom, in the form of Government agencies, banks, shops, even employers, they *are* you.

Set against all this fraud and misery for the victims of identity fraud, it's easy to see why most of us, most of the time, would welcome the activities of a company like Experian even if it does know everything there is to know about each of us: where we live, what we owe, where we shop, what we buy, how much we earn. And even if it does sell that information on to marketing companies which deluge us with booklets, catalogues, leaflets, appeals for money and so on. But if you want to buy a car, get a mortgage, acquire a new sofa or go on holiday and need to borrow money to do so, Experian will run credit checks on you for their clients.

According to Experian, as well as the petty con-merchants, our identities are being stolen to help fund terrorism, people-trafficking and drug trafficking. And identity theft is on the rise – in 2005, it cost the British economy £1.7 billion, up from £1.3 billion the year before with 82 per cent of cases not even reported to the police. Of the remaining 18 per cent, only seven per cent were actually prosecuted – that works out at 1.27 per cent of all identity theft cases.

Elderly people are among the most vulnerable victims. Helen Lord of Experian says: "People will actually take on the identity of elderly people, people with dementia and so on. We have seen examples of people being put into nursing homes so their identities can be stolen. But when we see someone called Edith who was born in 1972 we know something is not quite right." Equally loathsome is the theft of the identity of dead people. In 2005, no fewer than 82,000 deceased identities were stolen; 17,500 of these were from children under the age of 18. So how do terrorists use identity theft? They obtain a credit card – students are useful targets – then hand it over to a broker who, in turn, passes it on to people known in the trade as "bust-out merchants". These merchants put invented charges through on the stolen card. The payment is processed by the credit card company in good faith. The bust-out merchant hands the money over to the broker – minus his 10 per cent cut. The broker takes his fee then passes the rest of the money on to the terrorists' paymaster. He pays the cash into a bank account in a false name, in the name of a front business or a bogus charity. Using a Paypal internet account, the money is then transferred abroad to be used anywhere in the world. That, at least, is how they financed the 9/11 terrorist attacks on the twin towers, according to the FBI.

It's easy to steal your identity. If you move house someone can simply pick up your mail and pretend they're you. They even have your name on the electoral roll, they're probably still getting your utility bills. They might even receive your new credit card. It's often a problem with students and other young people who share the same address because it's so easy to pick up someone else's post.

Some frauds are a little more sophisticated. Con-men will ring credit card companies with your details and ask for new cards to be sent to a new address. Criminals may raid your dustbin and get enough information to take on your identity – after all, who shreds their bank statements and electricity bills before they chuck them away? Some gangs pay bin raiders £5 for one stolen letter. There's "shoulder surfing", where crooks watch as you put your PIN number into a machine. Bogus e-mails direct you to fake bank web-sites. Bogus callers claim to be from your bank and ask for identification information over the phone. And, of course, more and more of us are giving away all our details on the internet, or even over the phone, without any certainty that the people we're dealing with are honest. The advice from Experian is: Don't respond to cold calling, ensure post is re-directed when you move, register on the electoral roll immediately, shred all personal correspondence, don't respond to cold calling or e-mails, don't answer surveys, don't discuss personal details over the phone, monitor bank statements and get regular credit reports, and do not keep PIN numbers. That's asking a lot. But the alternative may be worse.

In 2003, 72-year-old pensioner Derek Bond was arrested at gunpoint and held in a South African jail for three weeks accused of a multi-million-dollar fraud in the USA. He was only released when the FBI finally conceded the Bristol Rotarian was not fraud suspect Derek Sykes, also known as Derek Bond, who had stolen his identity.

What this all means is we lose both ways. We have to accept there are enormous databases tracking our every move and we have to accept they are a necessary infringement of our right to privacy because the alternative is not merely that our own lives and identities are stolen but that they are then used to bring down Western civilisation.

It all sounds a little far-fetched but that's what's happening. Our lives are not our own. Privacy is something we can forget about. Big Brother is watching you. You are a number, not a free man.

The Conservatives are pledged to scrap the Government's identity card scheme if they win the next General Election. This alone should be reason enough to vote for them. It would at least relieve us of some of the State's oppression, save us some money as taxpayers and individuals and offer us back a little of our disappearing liberty.

David Davis, as Shadow Home Secretary, was rightly incensed that on the day Tony Blair unveiled his resignation timetable, the slippery Home Office sneaked out a new official cost for the Identity Card project. It said the new price was £5.30 billion – a rise of more than £600 million in less than a year. As Davis said: "It is no surprise the Government has had to revise their cost estimate up by so much. It undermines their criticism of the independent London School of Economics cost estimate of up to £20 billion. The public should brace themselves for more increases every time this estimate is updated. These cards will do nothing to protect our security and in fact may make it worse. Let us not forget that the Government's estimate does not take into account costs to be met by other Departments and has yet still to receive Treasury approval."

Sadly, scrapping identity cards, though a vital first step in deterring Big Brother from interfering in every aspect of our lives, will not remove the risks or give us back our real freedom because the surveillance society is both a private and a public sector phenomenon, its influence is every-where and there will be times when it is easier to submit to the thrall of a voluntary ID system than stand out against it and endure the many inconveniences which will result – from not being allowed on aeroplanes to being denied NHS treatment or State benefits.

The test of the Big Brother society is its effectiveness in protecting the innocent from crime. Most dramatically, it can be argued with much justification that the loss of our privacy is a small price to pay to be able to live in safety and walk the streets without fear. We have already seen how our surveillance society is not altogether effective in clearing the streets of crime but at least the police and secret services are protecting us from terrorist attack.

You would think, though, that with all the sophisticated and crude surveillance methods available to our guardians these days, they would be capable of making sure the people they go after are genuinely plan-ning a crime or guilty of one. Yet, notoriously, when two police officers shot Brazilian electrician Jean Charles de Menezes at point blank range on the London underground in 2005, it turned out they had got the wrong man. Not only did they mistake him for someone else and thus kill an innocent man, nobody was expected to take any responsibility for the murder.

The commander of the operation, Cressida Dick, was not called to account (indeed, she was promoted). Her boss, Head of the Metropolitan Police, the absurd Sir Ian Blair, got away Scot free not only with presiding over an illegal shoot-to-kill policy but also over an attempt to impede the Police Complaints Commission inquiry into the affair. The utter absurdity of the episode was seen in the fact that, rather than simply offer up a complete whitewash, the PCC decided to prosecute the police for breaching health and safety laws. How anyone could seriously regard the killing as a failure of health and safety policy is beyond comprehension, like accusing the Israeli army of racial discrimination at an industrial tribunal because they invaded Lebanon.

Big Brother may be watching. But Big Brother is incompetent. In the future, the real problems with the surveillance society won't come from criminals but from servants of the State, its semi-privatised agencies and private companies, using the information they hold about us to destroy our lives.

By mistake.

6
Gordon Brown and the cloak of invisibility

Britain is dead. The British don't exist. No less a person than the former Lord Chancellor, Lord Falconer, said so. As a Scot and a UK citizen he said he didn't feel "British". He made this stunning announcement on the day in 2006 when he declared as official Government policy that there would be no English Parliament – "not today, not tomorrow". Apparently, the English didn't want one and, even if they did, it would create a federal UK dominated by England, and that would never do.

The Lord Chancellor's views were surprising because some of his colleagues were trying to re-invent the idea of Britishness. They saw it as a useful cloak to spread over the many disparate groups, faiths, beliefs, ways of life and identities which go to make up the peoples of Great Britain. Like Harry Potter's, the aim of the cloak is to make these differences invisible. But it doesn't work.

The attempt to reinvigorate the concept of Britishness represents a politically-correct bid to revive a bogus national identity as a way of holding together an increasingly fragmented United Kingdom. Yet even as the concept is being encouraged by those who want everyone in these islands to share some kind of identity, there are more – notably the Scots, the Welsh, the Irish and, increasingly, the English – who are pulling in the opposite direction.

The four nations which were once the constituent parts of the United Kingdom, and the peoples who make up this artificial construct, don't want Britain any more. It was only ever a flag of convenience and it is a flag which may soon be struck. In future, we are likely to be citizens of our individual countries, or citizens of Europe, or both. But few of us are British by birth, inclination or tradition.

History will not help us define the British identity because, if it ever existed, it was only as a useful passport to power and possessions. It was never a matter of conviction or belief. And history is, of course, the problem. The year 2007 marked the 300th anniversary of the Act of Union which officially created Great Britain as a single entity; a United Kingdom, from the separate nations of Scotland and England. Wales had been part of the English kingdom for several hundred years; Ireland became part of the United Kingdom in 1801. For 250 years after 1707, it was reasonable to talk about a single United Kingdom of Great Britain.

Yet in all that time, the concept of Britain – and, therefore, of Britishness – was entirely artificial. It was a child of its time. Britain was created as a result of the rise of the Nation State as the most important entity in the emerging global politics. The Scots had to be bribed into dissolving their own parliament and accepting Anne as their Queen. The poet Robert Burns said his country had been "bought and sold for English gold". The Scots were penniless following a catastrophic attempt to build their own empire by colonising Panama. Many of Scotland's leading figures had poured money into this fruitless scheme. England bailed them out to the tune of £398,085 10s. Even so, there were violent demonstrations against the Union. Daniel Defoe wrote: "For every Scot in favour there is 99 against."

The union was christened in civil war. The Scots rose in Jacobite rebellions in 1715 and 1745. Subjugation of the people, industrialisation, enclosures, the embracing of the Scottish aristocracy, economic growth, prosperity, colonies, empires and new worlds to conquer – all combined to keep the union intact. Even so, the English – insofar as the inhabitants of England can be described as English – as the dominant force within Great Britain, have been obliged to limit their power and influence in order to accommodate their neighbours' demands. These days this is seen most notably in the excess of MPs from outside England sitting at Westminster, by the excessive per capita public spending lavished on these countries and by the ability of Scottish and Welsh MPs to vote on purely English affairs when there is no reciprocal arrangement for the English.

This systematic and deliberate diminution of the influence of the English is now a serious political issue, a bone of contention which needs urgent resolution. Yet it is against the interests of the Labour Party to make any significant changes. Which is why Lord Falconer ruled them out. But just as the concept of Britishness has been abandoned by the Scots, Welsh and Irish, so the English are also giving up on the idea.

Before 1707, nationhood in the British Isles was a distinctly parochial affair. The Scottish had their own Monarchy; the Irish had their aspirations to independence and religious freedom; the Welsh dreamed of the past. The English, who created the idea of Britishness, did so to justify their imperialism and encourage a sense of inclusiveness among, in particular, the Scots.

"The British identity" was a useful banner to raise at opportune moments throughout the days of the Empire and beyond, right up to the Second World War. It helped encourage the ambitious from the four separate nations to rally round and support the expansion of their collective power and influence at the round earth's imagined corners. The Union flag fluttered across an empire on which the sun never set. Yet the soldiers and administrators, conquerors, tradesmen and merchants, the entrepreneurs and millionaires whose adventures created and destroyed this empire were never in any real sense "British". They identified themselves by their homelands – even in the names they gave their new found lands, from New England and New South Wales to Nova Scotia, Perth and Dublin, South Australia.

As the empire faded, so the value of identifying oneself as "British" diminished. The tribal, nationalistic identities of the Scottish and Welsh – and more particularly, the Irish – reasserted themselves with increasing vehemence. From the Dublin uprising of 1916 and onwards, the pretence that the majority of the people of Ireland might ever consider themselves to be British was abandoned. The Protestants of Ulster continue to assert their allegiance to the idea yet, to most people in England, their declamations of loyalty are risible.

The growth of nationalism in Scotland and Wales, furthered and fostered by the establishment of a Parliament in the former and an Assembly in the latter, has more or less destroyed any sense of a unifying British identity in these two increasingly independent nation states.

They are, of course, able to demand their freedom from England because of the protection afforded by their membership of the European Union. The EU prefers to deal with smaller entities than nation states. Scotland, Wales and the two unequal parts of Ireland all more or less fulfil the EU's definition of a "region". They are, therefore, beneficiaries of Brussels' divide-and-rule policy which has successfully helped to diminish the role of traditional 19th century nations.

Britain was a product of the trend towards nation states which developed with the Industrial Revolution and the first wave of globalisation. This saw competition among Europeans to build empires and exploit the natural and human resources of the lands they took and held by force. Britain was constructed to encompass a multitude of mongrel races and nationalities in one simple description. It was particularly useful at the time of the Act of Union and has been ever since in creating a cover story for Monarchs imported to rule the country from Holland and Germany. They were scarcely in a position to embrace the identity of any constituent part of the United Kingdom so it was convenient all round to describe representatives of Houses of Orange or Saxe Coburg Gotha as "British".

Yet it is this very flexibility, the ability of Britishness to embrace every kind of ethnic, cultural and geographical idiosyncrasy, which has persuaded unscrupulous politicians to try to revive the idea of Britain for the 21st century. After all, if immigrant German Kaisers can call themselves British even when, like George I, they could not speak a word of English, why can't other, less fortunate, immigrants embrace the same concept and fly the same flag?

It is to accommodate the many diverse peoples who have arrived on the shores of Great Britain in the past 50 years or so that the concept of Britain has seen a late flowering. The inhabitants of the island have always had few unifying racial, genetic, cultural or even religious features. Today the position is less clear-cut than ever. More languages are spoken in London than in any other city in the world; the populations of big cities like Birmingham, Leicester and Bradford are increasingly non-white. Even the Conservative Party has abandoned the concept of "Christian values" on the grounds that the country can no longer be described as Christian.

There is an argument that these peoples need a unifying identity. They are British citizens. They may not be English, Welsh or Scottish but they are British. The national identity created to appease one ethnic minority – the Scottish – and used as a shield for many others, including Kings and Queens, is now available to describe the New British who would otherwise struggle to identify their nationalities and allegiances.

The British identity, which went out across the world to build an empire, has brought home with it a new generation of Britons whose beliefs, cultures, colours, identities and social lives have little in common with those who still make up a majority of the population.

Does this actually mean that, far from being dead, the British identity is enjoying a new lease of life; that history itself has turned full circle? The answer has to be no. Even though there are many people – an obvious example being the many black sportsmen and women who compete for Britain – who do identify themselves as British, we have to accept that the concept is out of date.

Like many of the countries left behind when the flag was run down on the Empire, Britain itself has no meaning any longer. It is not greater than the sum of its parts, largely because three of those parts – Scotland, Wales and Ireland – have given up on the whole idea. Britain must accept the logical consequence of devolution, which is dissolution.

In future, there is England and the English, not Britain and the British. The vast majority of "New Britons" may choose to describe themselves as such but, in reality, they are English, Scottish, Welsh or Irish not British.

It could be argued that Britain needs to be retained or even revived as the flag of convenience that embraces the New Britons living in the country. And while the desire for inclusivity is right and proper, it can only take place in the cultural and historical context of the creation and destruction of Great Britain, the nation state which served us well for 250 years or so.

Britain has been destroyed from within. The concept of Britishness no longer has any meaning for the vast majority of the people who live in England.

To describe yourself as British in the 21st century is to subscribe to a new form of apartheid made possible largely thanks to the petty parochialism of the Scottish. Their demands to go it alone have ensured the English no longer embrace Britain as a concept. It follows, therefore, that any new citizens of the countries of the United Kingdom will actually be doing themselves a disservice if they choose to describe themselves as British at a time when, otherwise, the whole concept has died out.

By doing so, they would be isolating themselves from the mainstream as much as if they were to cling onto a national identity based on where their families originated from. It could be argued that these countries are still "one nation" in their relationships with the rest of the world. Through Westminster, through the BBC and other media, through the 2012 Olympic Games in London, and through many other channels of communication and identity, the British nationality still holds good. Yet Britain is synonymous with England to most people.

The Scots, Welsh and Irish rebel against the very idea of Britishness; they reject the Union Flag; they object to the English language or an English accent. And they are free to express racism in terms which would be totally unacceptable in any other context – Welsh Nationalists call the English language "verbal foot and mouth disease"; Scottish Nationalists describe the Union Flag as "an oppressive symbol" or the "butcher's apron". So antagonistic are the Scots to the idea of Britain that they will not allow their soccer players to take part in the British team at the 2012

Olympics. As SNP leader and Scotland's "First Minister" Alex Salmond says, Britishness "went bust long ago" north of the border.

The concept of Britishness is most valuable these days not to the citizens of the countries involved in the United Kingdom but to politicians who aspire to rule this increasingly separatist and diverse collection of communities. Tony Blair felt the need to appoint his own "patriotism Minister" while Gordon Brown was obliged to mount his own appeal to British patriotism because of concern over his separatist roots. Laughably, he even went so far as to claim that one of his favourite football memories was a goal Paul Gascoigne scored for England against Scotland in Euro 96.

Among the many makeovers Mr Brown has subjected himself to has been swapping the Saltire for the Union Flag. It's no easy task. Mr Brown's appeal to patriotism is aimed at reinforcing the new image of these islands as tolerant, happy and multi-cultural. It seems churlish to refer to Dr Johnson's comment about patriotism being "the last refuge of the scoundrel" but there is something as phoney about it as there is about his forced smile which someone, somewhere, once persuaded him would be ingratiating rather than just grating.

Mr Brown says: "Instead of the BNP using (the Union flag) as a symbol of racial division, the flag should be a symbol of unity and part of a modern expression of patriotism too. All the United Kingdom should honour it, not ignore it. We should assert that the Union flag by definition is a flag for tolerance and inclusion."

The real aim is, of course, to win over the English. For the Scots and the Welsh, the value of Britishness has faded away. For Mr Brown, as for all other mainstream politicians, the Northern Irish are irrelevant because they don't vote for the same parties as everyone else, preferring home-grown fruitcakes of various descriptions.

It is the English Mr Brown must to win over; the same English who collectively voted Conservative at the 2005 General Election but still got a Labour administration; the same English who have for years suffered under the tyrannical yolk of Scottish rule. They hold the key to Mr Brown's future.

Yet it is the English who make Labour MPs so nervous. The Labour Party has never been happy with the idea of England. But it took a German, Gisela Stuart (MP for Birmingham Edgbaston) to say what so many of them think – that people who describe themselves as English are nothing but racists. In a widely-quoted article, Ms Stuart, suggested that calling yourself English was the equivalent of adopting what she called "extremist views offering simple certainties". In other words, she was equating an assertion of English national identity with an extremist, right-wing view of the world.

She claims: "At election time when I am attacked for being German, my vote goes up." This is not true because her vote has fallen consistently. As she is never attacked for being German, it's nothing to do with her nationality. But it may have something to do with Labour's attempts to undermine our national identity.

Ms Stuart was right to note the number of people describing themselves as English is on the rise. One of her arguments is that Britain is being undermined partly by the creation of an EU superstate. Surprisingly, her own enthusiasm for the European Union has waned in recent years, even though she was a member of the committee set up to create the constitution which has so far been rejected by both the French and Dutch. She notes that the rise of "Englishness" follows the creation of the Scottish parliament, the Welsh assembly and Government of England by a party, and a Cabinet, made up mainly of Scotsmen and women (by using a surname like Stuart, Gisela could easily be mistaken for a member of our ruling Scottish MacMafia).

She said: "The British identity is based on and anchored in its political and legal institutions and this enables it to take in new entrants more easily than if being a member of a nation were to be defined by blood."

There is so much wrong with this statement it's difficult to know where to start. She implies "the English" identify themselves as a separate racial bloodline when everyone knows we are a mongrel stock which has been raped, pillaged and plundered for centuries. She implies the rise of an English identity is somehow bound to create intolerance and racism. Yet it's the Scottish and Welsh whose anti-English racism and intolerance have been indulged by the Government and led to a backlash among the English. It is they, in their various different ways, who have rejected the concept of Britain – because they have been encouraged to do so by the divisive European Union and by Labour's need for votes.

Ms Stuart doesn't realise, perhaps, that the political and legal institutions she thinks so highly of are actually different in Scotland and in most of Ireland and have been for years. The English are victims of New Labour's constitutional racism. It is only natural we wish to protect ourselves from further humiliation and rejection by reasserting our real national identity. Ms Stuart will find the English are as welcoming and as tolerant as ever. And the continued decline in her vote will have nothing to do with racism. It's just that today the boot is on the other foot – powerful Scots trying to suborn their English subjects.'

Meanwhile Mr Brown can hardly declare himself English or even a supporter of, or lover of, England. So he does the next best thing and extols the virtues of Britain and the British. This is all-inclusive, politically correct and liable to offend nobody. Mr Brown cynically re-invents the cause of Britain to further his political career in exactly the same way that the concept has been manipulated since it was first established three centuries ago.

The snag is there are plenty of people in England who are now tired of "Britain" being used to justify the constant oppression of their country. Mr Brown's appeal to the Scottishness of his natural constituency and the Britishness of the English demonstrate once again that we are not one nation but four.

It is, of course, the English and only the English who can be discriminated against. This was seen in the summer of 2007 in the curious case of 18-year-old Abigail Howarth who was rejected by Environment Agency because she was too English. This bizarre story emerged at a time when the agency should have been up to its ears in flooding (and at a time when its top executives were trying to live down the huge bonuses they had recently rewarded themselves with). It prompted me to make some inquiries of my own. I was particularly eager to discover how the racism police discriminate between an Englishwoman and a white woman from elsewhere in the British Isles.

I thought, what about my wife? She was born Fiona Findlay, in Solihull, West Midlands, very close to Meriden, which is the centre of England. Her father George was born not that much further away, in Birmingham. Yet they both consider themselves to be Scottish. My wife's mother Sally was actually born in Glasgow though Sally's mother came from Devon. My wife's paternal grandparents came from the lowlands of Scotland. With that background, I wondered whether Fiona was Scottish enough to qualify for a job with the Environment Agency.

It is true that she fails the Tebbit test in that, when it comes to an international rugby match between Scotland and England, she backs the Scots. Yet the nationality of her parents is sufficiently ambiguous to suggest that she is, at the very least, qualified to play for England.

The Environment Agency had advertised for people of "Asian, Indian, White other (eg Irish, Welsh, Scottish, European), African, Caribbean or of Mixed Race origins" for a job in East Anglia. I wanted to know if Fiona was a "White other" or English and therefore wouldn't get the job. So, the question is: would Fiona qualify as "White other" when it came to seeking a job with the Environment Agency?

I asked the agency. They sighed. Then their spokesman, who is Australian – a "White other" if ever there was one – said: "Not us, guv." He said: "It's an anomaly in the law". He said: "We don't do the recruitment; we employ PATH to do that for us." So how does a white woman qualify as Scottish? "Ask PATH," he said, adding. "It's an anomaly."

PATH turns out to stand for Positive Action Training Highway. It's a business. It has an office in London and another in Birmingham. Its mission is to "address under-representation and inequalities of Black and minority ethnic groups in management and the professions through the provision of innovative training, career opportunities, motivation and support to individuals and organisations wishing to create a workforce that reflects our diverse communities."

In other words, its aim is to promote positive discrimination.

To justify its existence, it declares: "The term 'Positive Action' is used to describe measures under Sections 37 and 38 of the Race Relations Act (1976). The recent Race Relations Amendment Act (2000) imposes a general duty on listed public authorities, including government departments, the NHS, local authorities, governing bodies of publicly funded schools and colleges, The Housing Corporation, and police authorities. In carrying out their various functions organisations need to have due regard to the need to eliminate unlawful discrimination and to promote racial equality and good race relations. This means that they should take whatever steps are needed to ensure current policies and practices do not disadvantage any racial groups."

Inevitably, it has "partners". Inevitably, they are all public sector bodies happy if not eager to squander taxpayers' money on this kind of nonsense. They are: the Royal College of Midwives, the Planning Inspectorate, the "Equal Programme" (itself a quango of a quango of the EU), the Equalities and the Learning and Skills Council Provider Base (several quangos of a quango), the South East regional development agency and the "Pan-London Public Sector Employment Project".

I phone the Birmingham office and ask what definition of Scottish they're using. They sigh and tell me to ring Mary McDowell in London. She may even be Scottish herself, judging by the name. But I can't say whether she is or not because the telephonist asked who I was and what I wanted, sighed, went away, came back and said: "She's not available at the moment". "She says," I added. She laughed and denied it. I left my phone number. I never did get a response.

Meanwhile the Environment Agency also passed the buck to the Commission for Racial Equality where they also sighed when the subject was brought up and could not tell me what the definition of "Scottish" might be. Their only explanation was that if Fiona had described herself as Scottish in the last national census then she was Scottish. In other words, your ethnicity is entirely self-determined.

If you want to call yourself English, you can; if you think you're Scottish or Welsh or Irish, then you are. So really all poor Abigail Howarth had to do was decide that on the day she applied she was Welsh and she would have been. Which, of course, makes a mockery of the entire positive discrimination programme anyway. As if it needed any further mockery.

But it emphasises once again how the entire State of Britain is now founded on an institutional racism against the English.

The Dunfermline by-election in 2006 included the ironic sight of two Scottish politicians, Gordon Brown, then the British Chancellor of the Exchequer, and Douglas Alexander, then the British Secretary of State for Transport, condemning plans for higher tolls on the Forth Road Bridge even though, thanks to their own policies of devolution and fragmentation, they no longer had any responsibility for, or power over, such tolls. These same two Scottish MPs had the power to impose road tolls throughout England but had no say over the level or extent of tolls faced by their own constituents. This destruction of all-inclusive, British democracy has taken place over time but New Labour went out of its way to create an independent Scottish Parliament and divorce its supporters north of Hadrian's Wall from the rest of the country.

No Chancellor in history did more to assist the destruction of the United Kingdom of Great Britain and Northern Ireland than Mr Brown. Only when he saw the political risk of this to his own career did he start to back-pedal.

But it is too late. The only people who still call themselves British are Protestant Ulstermen and some people whose families have come from the old Commonwealth countries. Because the idea of Britain is dead among the majority of the population, those who cling onto the concept are in danger of identifying themselves as outsiders.

Britain is a superficially useful concept for unscrupulous politicians. But it's a slippery idea which has been destroyed not because of its historical associations, its "butcher's apron" flag or the inevitable dominance of England. It has been destroyed by the very people it was originally set up to protect and include in Britannia's protective embrace.

When we see Gordon Brown struggling to sell himself to the people of England, we must remember he has no-one to blame but himself. It was he and his party of Scotsmen who finally defeated the British.

Doubtless he is well aware that England voted Conservative but got Labour. By 8,086,306 votes to 8,028,512 the Labour Party lost in England in 2005 – yet Labour won 285 English seats to the Tories' 193. The Scots have excessive influence for a small country with a total population of 5,062,011, just eight per cent of the UK population. The West Midlands, by contrast, represents 10.7 per cent of the UK with 5,267,000 inhabitants.

Imagine if the entire United Kingdom were run by the West Midlands. We'd get the best of everything and the rest of the country would have to wait. We could give our students free education while charging everyone else up to £3,000 in tuition fees. We could build ourselves new hospitals, roads and schools at vast expense and then let everyone else make do and mend.

Obviously we would build ourselves a huge and prestigious new head-quarters at ten times the originally-quoted cost. But mainly we would make sure that our political leaders kept all the best jobs for their fellow West Midlanders. The corridors of power would echo to the Black Country accent, which would become compulsory for all BBC TV and radio newsreaders. Of course the rest of the country might resent this take-over by the West Midlands but as there are more people living in the West Midlands than in the whole of Scotland, why not introduce rule from Wolverhampton?

It occurred to me that this could be the answer when John Reid, then a Cabinet Minister, fell out with BBC presenter Jeremy Paxman who complained that England was being ruled by "the Scottish Raj". Dr Reid complained Paxman was being snobbish and whined: "If you have a PhD and a posh accent from a school like yours (Paxman went to Malvern College), you are regarded as a sophisticate."

The Scottish Raj seized control of our Government. Reid was just one representative of the MacMafia, the existence of which proves once again the truth of Lichfield sage Dr Johnson's words 250 years ago when he said: "The noblest prospect a Scotsman ever sees is the high road that leads him to England."

True, the number of Scots MPs was cut from 72 to 59 in recognition of the fact that they have their own Parliament. But even so, why should they be allowed to carry on voting for laws which don't apply to their own country and do apply in England? You might think this is all a bit academic. But Tony Blair was only able to get Parliament to impose "top up" fees for students going to university by relying on the votes of Scottish MPs to overwhelm the backbench rebels representing English constituencies. That piece of law only got through parliament with a majority of five. Without the Scottish vote, it would have been thrown out, as it deserved to be. The great irony isn't simply that Scottish MPs imposed this charge on English students – they did so safe in the knowledge that tuition fees are not imposed on students at Scottish universities (except if they're from England, of course, when they have to pay up).

This is such a grossly unfair situation that it is no longer defensible. Cutting the number of Scottish MPs isn't a good enough answer. England needs the freedom to make its own laws and escape from the thrall of the Scots once and for all.

The influence of the Scots has been totally out of proportion for centuries. Since the introduction of Parliamentary reform in 1832, we've had 29 Prime Ministers and a wholly excessive eight of them were Scottish. Gordon Brown would be wise to appoint a Secretary of State for England and establish a rule in Parliament that only English MPs vote for English laws.

It won't solve the bias in the system that gives the Tories more votes in England and Labour more seats. But it would be a start. If home rule works for the Welsh, the Scots and the Irish then it's about time it worked for the English as well.

After Scotland voted, marginally, for a nationalist-led coalition in Edinburgh at the 2007 elections, there was a greater chance of a referendum on independence. This would, we must assume, be decided on by a majority of the Scots. But if the union were to be dissolved, then both parties to the agreement should be given a say in its future. Each party should decide if it wished to abandon the agreement.

When push comes to shove, the Scots may suddenly realise which side their bread is buttered and bottle out rather than choose independence. But if they were to have a vote on union, the English should be given one as well. Do the English wish to maintain the union with Scotland or do we think it's a constitutional arrangement whose time has come? If the answer is that we do not wish to retain the union then we should cast the Scottish adrift and make them fend for themselves whether they want to or not. It takes two to make a union but only one to break it – why should it only ever be the Scots who are consulted on this question?

I wrote as much in an article in the Wolverhampton *Express & Star* and received all manner of abusive and threatening e-mails sent anonymously from Scotsmen who do not like the idea that the English should have a say in this issue. But if Gordon Brown wins a General Election in his own right, this is an issue which cannot be dismissed as simply a domestic issue in his own, Scottish, back-yard.

7
Vote early, vote often

It's astonishing how easy it is to rig an election in this country. There are so many possibilities...

For a start, there's nothing to stop anyone registering as an elector in more than one place at the same time. I know of one MP who was registered at three separate addresses at the time of the last General Election. Obviously it's illegal to vote twice or more but if you wanted to break the law, the chances are very good indeed that you would get away with it. Who would ever check? It may be somewhat inconvenient to whizz round a single constituency – or even half way across the country – to vote several times on election day, but it's possible. Much easier is to do the same thing by post, exercising your right to a postal ballot.

Better still, though, is the possibility of registering one or more bogus residents in your house and then voting on their behalf as well. The average semi could easily accommodate a dozen people without the local council's elections department bothering to check whether they actually exist or not. It's also possible to collect other people's postal vote forms and offer to return them to the elections office on their behalf. While in your possession, you could make sure the votes are cast for the candidate of your – as opposed to the original voter's – choice.

There's also proxy votes to bear in mind. A quick tour of an old folk's home could easily yeild several dozen opportunities for you to vote for your favoured candidate as a stand-in for the actual voter. This is legal on a one-to-one basis but industrial-strength proxy voting is entirely possible, especially if you know the people in charge of the home and they have similar political views to your own.

There are probably a dozen more ways of cheating the system on top of these, if you have a sufficiently devious or ingenious approach to the problem of getting people to vote for you. But whenever the dangers have been pointed out to the Government it has chosen to say that a bit of election fraud is a price worth paying if more people are going to vote.

Specifically the Government has made it laughably easy for us all to use a postal vote. There are some good reasons for this. We may be on holiday or away on business on election day. We may be unable to make it to the polling station. We might forget what day polling takes place. For all these reasons, a postal vote can be a valuable extension of democracy. But that doesn't stop it being open to widespread abuse.

As a country which regularly sends observers off around the world to pronounce on the legitimacy or otherwise of other people's elections, and as a country which trains aspiring foreign politicians in the delights of democracy, we presumably have an obligation to keep our own squeaky clean.

Yet it has been obvious for a long time that the voting system is not foolproof. When I stood at the 2001 General Election there were some very overcrowded homes on the electoral register which seemed fairly empty whenever we canvassed them. We couldn't prove anything and even if there had been a bit of vote-rigging it wouldn't have affected the outcome. But at a closely-fought election it might easily tip the balance in favour of one candidate rather than another.

Richard Mawrey, QC, the Election Commissioner, investigated claims of "widespread corrupt and illegal conduct" against six Labour councillors in Birmingham. Interestingly the Labour Party tried to put off his inquiry until after the 2005 General Election.

But Mr Mawrey warned that if he found the allegations of vote-rigging to be proved, it meant the entire postal vote system was open to abuse and would have to be reformed. He said: "We are not dealing with a frolic by a number of hotheads. The allegation is that there is a pattern throughout the Birmingham area of impropriety in relation to at least the election of Labour Party candidates. If the allegations are correct, then the current system of postal voting is open to abuse and serious fraud. If that's the case, then it's clearly essential that this is known well before the possible general election."

So what happened? Mr Mawrey warned the Government before the 2005 General Election was called that the results couldn't be trusted. The High Court Judge found six Labour councillors guilty of electoral fraud in Birmingham and said they were responsible for a "massive, systematic and organised fraud" that would "disgrace a banana republic". More to the point, he said the electoral system was "hopelessly insecure" and said there were "no systems to deal realistically with fraud and there never have been. Until there are, fraud will continue unabated."

The Chief Executive of Birmingham City Council at the time was Lin Homer. She was subsequently promoted to run the even-more-disastrous Immigration and Nationality Directorate (on a salary of £200,000 a year).

During the investigation, Ms Homer was accused of failing to discharge her duties in accordance with electoral law. Judge Mawrey said she "threw the rule book out of the window" to deal with overwhelming numbers of postal vote application forms received. The judge complained: "Postal ballot packages are sent out by ordinary mail in clearly identifiable envelopes. Short of writing 'Steal Me' on the envelopes, it is hard to see what more could be done to ensure their coming into the wrong hands."

In her defence, Ms Homer denied responsibility, claiming she was only in "strategic, not operational control". Her role was confined to "motivational management and fire fighting". She left Birmingham soon after the 2005 General Election, when fears of fraud again surfaced. She calmed our fears by declaring that "virtually all" the 39,000 postal votes received were genuine. Note the use of the word "virtually" here. Note also that the city council issued 59,000 postal votes and only received back 39,000. What happened to the other 20,000? Who can tell? Certainly not Ms Homer.

A little local scandal involving a few councillors in inner city wards could be dismissed as more or less insignificant. Yet it amounted almost to officially-sanctioned vote-rigging. George W Bush's first term of office as US President was dogged by claims that he came to power illegally. It does matter that Western democracies are not only open and honest but are seen to be.

Yet at the 2005 General Election, there were many results which could have been influenced by a little judicious vote-rigging. We cannot be positive that it was won, fair and square, by the Labour Party even though it probably was.

One of the most remarkable outcomes of the election was the number of seats which were won and lost with very small majorities. In most seats most of the time, the winner gets in with a decent majority. Certainly something in four figures. And it's hard to believe it is possible that even sustained and determined electoral fraud could influence the outcome sufficiently to engineer a majority of more than 1,000 (though even that has to be possible given that in Birmingham alone some 20,000 postal votes went "missing"). But when a winning majority falls below about 1,000 then maybe the ability of a fraudster to swing an election has to be taken seriously.

There were plenty of results all over the country where it had to be at least possible the swing had nothing much to do with the views of the voters. Thousands of students had two votes. They were registered at home and at university and, though it's illegal, nobody would find out if they used both votes. Votes were stolen – when broadcasters John Humphries and Mariella Frostrup turned up to vote, they found someone else had already done so, by post, in their names. In many cases, houses filled with more adults than most of us could stand living with under one roof, spawned a dozen or so postal votes. Yet when anyone tried to speak to any of these eager voters, they had disappeared. It could be that's why they wanted postal votes in the first place – because they were all going away on holiday to escape the hype of the election. But it might be that they never existed in the first place and that some unscrupulous fixer has invented them to boost the campaign of his chosen politician.

Obviously nobody knows the full extent of the fraud at the 2005 General Election. How could they? That's the point of fraud – it's criminal but you do it if you think you can get away with it. And with the electoral system – especially the postal vote scandal but not just that – vulnerable to cheating, we cannot be certain that any result is entirely legitimate.

There were serious claims of fraud in Birmingham Ladywood, where Clare Short won with a majority of 6,801. Jack Straw was re-elected in Blackburn with a majority of 8,009 so even though postal voters in his constituency were among "the disappeared". But what about Hereford where the Lib Dem won with a majority of 962? Or Solihull where the Lib Dem majority was just 279? Or Stourbridge which Labour won by 407 votes? Or Warwick and Leamington, won by Labour with a majority of 306? Or The Wrekin which the Tories took by 942? The ability to swing a seat by indulging in electoral fraud is much greater where the winning margin is modest. Yet we seem to have come to accept this as a hazard of the system.

Exposés of dirty dealings – usually, but not always – by the Labour Party, appear in the papers with monotonous regularity. They make headlines in papers like the "Express & Star" in Wolverhampton or in the "Sunday Times". Yet, remarkably, few prosecutions result and little effort is made to reform the system or tackle fraud.

Interestingly, the postal vote system – the most likely source of fraud – was defended by the Government on the basis that it encouraged a higher turnout. That argument did not stand up to scrutiny – turnout at 61.3 per cent in 2005 was up all of two per cent on 2001 but that's hardly proof of the benefits of widespread postal voting. Especially when set against the potential disadvantage that the will of the people is being subverted by criminals.

There are cruder methods as well. I know of Labour candidates who intimidate the elderly into handing over their postal vote ballot papers and allowing the party activists to fill them in. I have seen official tellers at election counts celebrate Labour victories in local elections even before the results have been disclosed to the candidates. I have even seen the distinctly fishy sight of tellers opening about 100 ballot papers and discovering that each and every one of them carries a cross against the name of the Labour candidate in a closely-fought ward contested by four people. It is not possible to say that in any of these instances that electoral fraud had definitely taken place. But the smell of corruption lingered long after the returning officer announced the results. And it will continue to cast a pall over this country's elections in the future.

Then there are experiments with electronic voting, the use of computer scanners to verify ballots, and even on-line elections – all fraught with difficulties. Yet the Labour Government habitually ignores advice over how to prevent corruption and confusion at elections – resulting in the disgraceful scandal of no fewer than 100,000 spoilt ballot papers at the Scottish elections of 2007. That represented 10 per cent of the votes cast, in effect invalidating the entire election, in which the Scottish National-ists emerged as largest party in the Edinburgh parliament with a majority of one.

The best days of democracy – the days of honesty – seem to be behind us. Whoever wins future elections, can we trust the results? It's doubtful.

8
The sick man of England

Disturbing news from my local doctors' surgery: They've introduced appointment cards sponsored by a firm of undertakers.

The cards are scarcely necessary as it's almost impossible to get an appointment anyway – but these have got advertisements on the back. No doubt this is part of the commercialisation of the National Health Service and all very entrepreneurial. But is it really necessary for the ads to include one for the local funeral director's? It doesn't fill us patients with a great deal of confidence. Maybe it's the latest ploy to cut waiting lists. If you draw the patient's attention to the services of an undertaker they may not feel so poorly after all.

The ads, if not the undertakers, are a sign of what is happening to the NHS. The Government is being accused of handing it over to the private sector. Can this possibly be true? And would it be wrong if it were? In 2006, the country's hospitals were more than £1 billion in the red. According to the doctors' trade union, the British Medical Association, three-quarters of all hospitals were short of money and one third were imposing cuts, ranging from £200,000 to £25 million.

The BMA blames the Government's decision to hand much of the work previously carried out by the NHS to privately-run businesses – known in the jargon as Independent Sector Treatment Centres. They concentrate on apparently straightforward operations like cataract removal, endoscopy, hernia repair, removal of fibroids, abortion, removing tonsils, knee surgery and varicose vein surgery. These centres are springing up all over the place. The Department of Health says they will "help provide the extra clinical capacity needed to deliver swift access to treatment for NHS patients; spearhead diversity and choice in clinical services for NHS patients; and stimulate innovative models of service delivery and drive up productivity".

You know as soon as you see words like "spearhead" and "drive up" that you are facing the usual bureaucratic drivel. The aim is to cut waiting lists by getting round the NHS bureaucracy. It may work. A survey of five of these private sector clinics carried out for the Government said that out of 13,000 operations, only three had been cancelled for non-clinical reasons. The NHS will never be able to match that for patient service. The snag is, though, that critics are queuing up to blame all NHS overspending on this scheme. They call it privatisation, even though it isn't. Proper privatisation would mean patients paying directly for their treatment – under this scheme it still comes free, it's just provided more efficiently.

To make it attractive to the private sector, the NHS, in its dumb bureaucratic stupidity, made some serious mistakes. It agreed to guarantee a certain number of patients for these treatment centres and agreed to pay guaranteed prices for each treatment. Even better for the private businesses, the NHS is paying up front and over the odds for operations which may never even take place. To help find the money, critics allege, public sector hospitals are made to cut their provision. But obviously they would have to do so anyway if their bread-and-butter patients were being sent elsewhere. It seems the private clinics may improve patient care but they may also reduce the amount of money the NHS has available to pay for existing hospitals.

At a cost to the taxpayer of £4.5 billion, the clinics may be one cause of the huge deficits built up by hospitals across the country. But it's not the only one, or even a major part of the problem. The centres are just a useful stick for trade unions and others with a vested interest in the status quo to beat the Government with.

It is hard to believe that a service like the NHS, which has had so much money poured into it for such a long time, cannot cope with the demands placed upon it. But that is, indeed, the case.
We love the NHS because it sees us through from the cradle to the grave, and at some point it will care for everyone we know and love. Even those who would rather go private, and could afford to do so, know very well

that they need the State health system if they are knocked down by a bus, if they discover a severe cancer or they have a heart attack – for serious, expensive, long-term or emergency care in England, there is only one place to go, the NHS. We are duly grateful and revere the service and its supposed egalitarianism. And when it comes to getting the best out of the service, we all have a highly-personal vested interest in demanding more and better. We are less likely to seek "value for money" from the NHS than from just about any other service provided by the public or private sectors because we know that one day it will swallow up our own feeble bodies and those of our loved ones. This is personal. It is impossible to contemplate the service objectively because we all have personal experiences, and if it goes well, we are suitably grateful and supportive. That's why nurses – many of whom are anything but – still tend to be described in the tabloids and the popular imagination as "angels".

So the service lurches from crisis to crisis, from scandal to scandal, without let or hindrance because nobody, but nobody, has the courage to say the King is not wearing any clothes. The NHS is a scandal and nobody is willing to admit it, let alone do anything about it. The organisation is supposedly the third largest employer in the world, after the Red Army in China and the Indian railways. Yet we fail to recognise that it is a monster of inefficiency, complacency and arrogance.

Since 1997, the amount of taxpayers' money pumped into the NHS almost trebled, from £33 billion to £92.6 billion in 2007-8. That, in itself, was originally expected by New Labour to be enough to solve most of its problems. But half the increase disappeared in higher salaries to existing staff. Admittedly, there were some more doctors and nurses but the biggest staffing increase was in the 71 per cent more managers employed under New Labour.

Some of the money went on the Independent Sector Treatment Centres (ISTCs) but only £4.5 billion. More – much, much more – is being spent on a new computer system for the entire health service. Estimates of what this may cost by the time it's finished, if it is ever finished, range from £3 billion to over £31 billion.

A new internal market to pay for NHS treatment, aimed at increasing patient choice, has generated a whole new paper-chasing bureaucracy. And what improvements are there in the way patients are treated? Some waiting lists are shorter – though some of them have been fiddled to make them look better than they really are. Infections caught at hospital have increased dramatically and so have the number of operations cancelled at the last minute for non-medical reasons. Meanwhile patients have died because the nurses recruited from Third World countries cannot speak English and, as Tony Blair found out during the 2005 General Election campaign, it's now almost impossible to obtain an appointment with a GP more than two days in advance.

The biggest crisis is in hospitals, however. Up and down the country, wards are being shut, services withdrawn, staff laid off. In spite of record levels of spending by the Government, many hospitals are up to their ears in debt.

In 2006, the Royal Wolverhampton Hospitals NHS Trust said it would be £37 million in the red by March 2008 even if a £20 million saving plan worked; Mid Staffordshire General Hospitals NHS Trust was trying to save £6 million; in Worcestershire the figure was £20 million; in Shrewsbury and Telford was £36 million. Sandwell Hospital's new £20 million accident and emergency centre was earmarked for closure. Good Hope Hospital in Sutton Coldfield was strapped for cash to the tune of £20 million. In Coventry they were a mere £7.8 million short; in Warwick it was £8.5 million. Hospitals in the West Midlands were collectively in the red to the tune of well over £100 million. Across the country the figure being bandied about originally was £250 million for the entire NHS. Within weeks, it rocketed to £1 billion.

The hospitals shut down premises, axing accident and emergency services, not replacing staff, laying people off, making nurses redundant, doing without consultants. They postponed operations and hoped the patients died quickly, without anybody noticing that lack of NHS treatment was the cause. They amalgamated, cut, shelved, closed, reduced, mothballed and retrenched until the books looked a little healthier. But why was the situation so grave? How is it possible, when the amount of taxpayers' money poured into the NHS has more than doubled, that our hospitals were so desperately short of money? Some experts claimed the NHS was facing "the worst crisis in its history".

One answer can be found in an Office for National Statistics report claiming productivity in the NHS may actually have fallen between 1995 and 2003 by one per cent or, at best, stayed the same. Waiting lists were falling – but partly, at least, because many hospitals lied about them, according to the National Audit Office. The number of operations cancelled at the last minute was rising while deaths from bugs caught in hospital rose fifteen-fold between 1993 and 2002. In the midst of all this came yet another reorganisation of the way the health service is run. Tony Blair called it "much-needed reform"; his critics called it "wholesale privatisation". Either way, it's doubtful we were getting the kind of health service most people expected when Labour claimed the NHS was only safe in his hands and the voters had "24 hours to save the NHS".

Gordon Brown led us all to believe the liberal application of money to all the diseased parts of the health service would somehow cure the illnesses. If anything, it made the fever worse. One reason is simple: a great deal of the money disappeared paying existing staff more to do the same old jobs. That is not greater productivity or better patient care; it's simply buying off the loyal Labour voters who work for the NHS.

Yes, there are more nurses and doctors. You can't get an appointment with a GP these days but there are more of them about. They are better paid than ever before but, thanks to the stupidity of Labour's negotiators, they do less work than ever before.
As for nurses, the snag is that many of them were trained abroad and don't speak English – a potentially fatal drawback as a Manchester coroner noted when he declared a patient had died through "lack of basic care" from nurses who couldn't understand the language.

Paying people more money to do the same jobs is only part of the problem. Another is that the Government reduced the working hours of doctors, thus forcing the NHS to employ more people to do the same amount of work. This may be right and proper from the point of view of an overworked doctor but – unless tired housemen really did kill their patients – it doesn't treat a single extra patient. For huge chunks of the extra money we, the taxpayers, are pouring into the NHS, we get little in return except cuts and closures.

The people who run our hospitals, the administrators who get blamed when it comes to "cuts" and who have to look coldly at the accounts and say where the money is haemorrhaging away, have few options. They get told what pay rises to give their staff, from the cleaners to the consultants. There is hardly any room for local manoeuvre or negotiation. And whatever the headline scandals we read about the cost of a course of anti-cancer drugs, the biggest overhead in the NHS is its employees – by a country mile.

Half of all the extra billions poured into the NHS went on pay. The service's wages and salary bill soared by a stunning £21.5 billion between 1997 and 2005. Admittedly it employed more people – up from 1,059,000 in 1997 to 1,331,000 in 2005 (though even that is misleading because tens of thousands of people only work part-time). The statistics are telling, though, and give us some insight into why our hospitals are now being forced to save a fortune. The number of GPs employed by the NHS has increased 16 per cent. On the other hand, the number of bureaucrats, managers and pen-pushers has soared by 71 per cent.

The money is also going in other ways: on the massive pension bills for NHS staff who still get to retire at 60; a new consultants' contract, which was more expensive than the Government expected; a new contract for GPs which was much more expensive than the Government expected; a drugs bill rising way above the rate of inflation; costs linked to the EU working time directive, which means that many more staff must be employed to undertake the same work as before.

The somewhat eccentric medical MP, Wyre Forest Health Concern's Dr Richard Taylor, says there have been 14 NHS re-organisations since Labour took power in 1997. In effect the NHS is undergoing perpetual change, which means the staff can't concentrate on the job of treating patients properly because they have to deal with the latest Government fad. And, of course, every re-organisation costs money.

One of the latest ways of squandering our money is the dubious idea of a national computer system for all our patient records. The NHS is getting a new, all-singing, all-dancing computer system which will supposedly provide on-line records for 50 million patients by 2010. One morning I rang the Department of Health to check on the latest score.

"Why do you want to know?" they asked suspiciously. It took them until lunch-time to come back with the answer £6.2 billion. I replied: "But the BBC said a year ago that it might cost anything between £18.6 billion and £31 billion." They stuck to the number they first thought of, though it seems nobody really knows how much it will cost. My money is on being a lot closer to £31 billion than £6 billion.

The NHS isn't the only Government department to squander billions on computer systems which don't work properly. A survey in 2002 said only 28 per cent of all IT projects in America are on budget, on time and work while 23 per cent are abandoned altogether. The NHS computerisation plan, the largest civil IT programme this country has ever seen, is looking poorly. It's months behind schedule. There is a growing fear that if the system does go way over budget, local health trusts will have to pick up the bill. Ministers have promised it won't happen. But then their department still claims the true cost will only be £6.2 billion.

The system has already led to an accounts scandal at iSoft, one of the companies working on the project. iSoft, which made heavy losses and has been under investigation by the Financial Services Authority, was forced to sack Steve Graham, its co-founder and commercial director, and lost Ravi Kumar, its chief technology officer. The business was twice bailed out by the Government to the tune of £82 million as it struggled to develop its software. A Commons Public Accounts Committee report said: "We are concerned in particular that iSoft's flagship software product, 'Lorenzo' – on which three fifths of the programme depends – is not yet available despite statements from the company in its 2005 annual report that the product was available from early 2004."

It is worth noting at this point that the ex-boss of the CBI, Digby Jones – now styling himself Digby, Lord Jones of Birmingham since becoming Gordon Brown's Minister for Trade Development – was a director of iSoft. While as the director general of the CBI he was trying to impress on company directors their responsibilities – especially those non-executives who see a seat on the board as a lucrative sinecure – he was apparently ignorant of the problems at the company where he was himself employed as a non-executive.

Lord Jones was a director of iSoft for five years and when the company came under investigation for accountancy irregularities, our fearless hero declared: "There is a limit to what a non-executive can know. They have to rely on what advisers tell them and what the executive team tells them. It is important that people understand this."

He rejected claims that he helped cover up early signs of the problems even though, according to the *"Daily Telegraph"*, he is "understood to have been present at a key meeting of the company's audit committee where discussions took place over the correct accounting treatment for revenue that was received from ongoing contracts. The meeting was also held in his offices at the CBI, but Jones was no longer an active member of the audit committee and is understood to have been present only briefly, in an advisory capacity. According to one source close to iSoft, the company's accountants were asked to say where its accounting treatment would lie on a scale of 1 to 10 – where 1 is ultra conservative and 10 is legal but aggressive. It was told they were a 6 or 7."

Inevitably, Lord Jones deflected any blame by trying to "encourage a more realistic understanding of the role of non-executives". He said: "We have all got PhDs in hindsight and if you ask me whether I have enjoyed seeing my name associated with this all summer, then the answer is no. There were many other people involved who don't get their names mentioned." Yes, Minister, but few of them take the Brown shilling and set themselves up as business gurus. The new, computerised, know-everything NHS will, of course, be a financial disaster – and when it's finished we can be absolutely certain that security will be non-existent. If the NHS computer system has your medical records on it, you can be sure that information will be made available to a wide range of official, semi-official and illegal agencies. For a fee. Patient confidentiality is very expensively being thrown out of the window in the name of an efficiency which will probably never materialise.

Meanwhile, hospitals are killing their patients. The scare stories about super-bugs are so rife some hospitals should carry a health warning. Every patient represents a triumph of hope over experience as the creaking National Health Service tries to keep body and soul together for just a little longer.

I had to rush my 17-year-old niece into Warwick Hospital at midnight when the wounds where her recently-removed tonsils used to be became infected. She was bleeding alarmingly. She was immediately re-admitted to the ward she had already been re-admitted to once before.

Naturally the doctors were busy so it took three hours for anyone to see her. When they did, her notes were missing so nobody knew the dosage of antibiotics she was on. They had to take another blood sample because the results of the last one had gone astray as well. The distress of the patient was made worse by the fact that the first time they extracted blood from her arm they didn't take enough so they had to go through the same rigmarole all over again.

Finally she was put to bed. Except that the duvet cover, supposedly clean because it looked freshly pressed, was vile. It had what may have been bird droppings on it together with stray hairs stuck to the stuff. It was, to use my niece's favourite word, "rank". There were drops of blood on the wall next to her bed. Someone had tried to wash it off but hadn't done a very thorough job. The whole ward contained only three patients – all of them teenagers, all of them re-admitted after their wounds became infected. This may be coincidence but you do start to worry, especially when, for no apparent reason, the place smells like an old people's home. There was certainly no whiff of disinfectant.

The nurses try to help. The doctors go through the motions. But all the time you keep thinking about the frequent reports of filthy hospitals and dangerous new diseases. It's no fun watching a teenager in tears as the pain and fear of illness strikes. It's even worse when you can't summon up the confidence you think you should have in the system that's supposed to be looking after her. Who's to blame? It's nothing to do with money. The hospital is fairly new and seems reasonably well-equipped. It's not a lack of staff. There were more nurses on duty in the ward than there were patients. But there really does seem to be a lack of hygiene and a terrible inefficiency.

A great friend of mine was horribly injured in a car crash. He was taken to Worcestershire Royal Hospital. The hospital was virtually brand new, having opened in March 2002 at a cost of £95 million under the much-vaunted but financially dubious Private Finance Initiative. Its development led, among other things, to the battle over Kidderminster Hospital and the election of Dr Taylor. It has nine operating theatres, 550 beds, and a £4 million training centre. It was to this all-singing, all-dancing facility that my friend was rushed with his life in severe danger. With diligence, care and skill the medical staff saved his life and two weeks later he was bored enough lying in his hospital bed to persuade the hospital staff that he'd be better off being cared for by his wife and family back home in Malvern.

He was discharged and spend one day and one night at home. By the following day, however, he was in serious trouble. Filled with aches and pains. Sweating and feverish. He was whisked back to the hospital where he died the same day. Of an infection he had caught during his time in hospital recuperating from his life-saving operation. If that isn't an example of the terrible waste of today's NHS I don't know what is. The staff use all their powers to save a life and it's lost anyway because a brand new hospital is so unhygienic that its patients get infected and die.

A few days after Gordon Brown called off the 2007 General Election (of which more later), the results of an inquiry into deaths at Maidstone and Tunbridge Wells NHS Trust in Kent were announced and scandalous they were too. The Healthcare Commission said at least 90 patients had died from clostridium difficile, a nasty little germ which flourishes on filth. C.difficile is a hospital-acquired infection which usually causes diarrhoea but can lead to fevers, severe inflammation, and death in around five per cent of cases. Older people are particularly at risk, but people aged 45-64 are also vulnerable – a quarter of all cases occur in under-65s.

The Maidstone and Tunbridge Wells investigators looked into 345 deaths between April 2004 and September 2006 and concluded that C.difficile was definitely or probably the main cause of death for 90 patients. It contributed to the deaths of another 124 people and may have been a factor in a further 55 cases – a total of 269 people who may have died as a result of a hospital-borne infection which would have been avoided if doctors and nurses were only prepared to wash their hands properly in soap and water. Another 1,100 or so patients were infected with the disease – but they, at least, didn't die.

The details made grim reading. It was claimed nurses did not have time to wash their hands properly. They left bed-bound patients, who were suffering from diarrhoea, to fend for themselves. They had to stew in their own juices while wards which, in a different era, would have smelled of disinfectant and carbolic, smelled instead of lavatories. The disgusting images this conjures up are too repulsive to contemplate for long. Squalor is the only word to describe it.

According to the experts, the best way to tackle the infection is simple: wash the rooms and your hands with warm water and detergent. It doesn't require much money nor does it take much time – which is why excuses that the nurses were over-worked and the management were too worried about balancing the books don't cut much ice. Even the consultants failed to take basic hygiene precautions.

This is the 21st century. In a previous era hospitals may not have had many sophisticated machines to aid their patients but they had bossy matrons and harassed staff who were forced on pain of death to keep their wards spotlessly clean. Today that is simply not true and the net result is the rise and rise of hospital-borne infections – the Health Protection Agency said there were 42,625 cases of C.difficile infection in patients aged 65 years and above in England in the first three quarters of 2006 a rise of 5.5 per cent on same period in the previous year.

Cases have been rising at an alarming rate. The number of cases reported to the Health Protection Agency increased from less than 1,000 in the early 1990s to 22,000 in 2002, 28,000 in 2003 and 44,488 in 2004. Some of this was due to improved diagnostic tests and improved reporting by laboratories, but, as the Department of Health admits, "there has clearly been a very significant increase in the number of cases".

If ever there were a need to get "back to basics" it's in the National Health Service. How can we carry on pouring money into an organisation which is so ineffective it neglects the most basic aspects of health care and therefore infects the very people it is trying to make better? Some people blame the privatisation of hospital cleaning for this scandal. But even if there were any truth in the allegation, it implies there is nobody in the entire army of NHD staff who can be bothered enforce basic hygiene standards not just on cleaners but on care workers, nurses and even consultants?

One of the tenets of the medical profession is the Hippocratic Oath, supposedly first drawn up by Hippocrates, the "father of medicine" in the fourth century BC. One of the first requirements made of any doctor who swears this oath is: "To practice and prescribe to the best of my ability for the good of my patients, and to try to avoid harming them." Every day, our hospitals are breaking the Hippocratic Oath.

9
The London Tax just won't wash

There is no doubt we have to build more houses. That's partly because we live longer so there are more widows and widowers in need of single-person accommodation. It's partly because we get married later and keep getting divorced, so a household of two adults and 2.4 children now needs two roofs over its head instead of one. But it's mainly because the population is booming as a result of more or less unrestricted immigration.

We allow 500,000 more immigrants every year into Britain. The population is expected to increase by five million to 65 million by 2025 and hit 71 million by 2050. Put a stop to illegal immigration and sent bogus asylum-seekers home and we wouldn't need the biggest house-building programme in history. But as Gordon Brown seems incapable of any restraint on the number of people who are allowed into the country, it's obvious they need somewhere to live.

Some of this development could actually enhance the countryside. As the late, great Nicholas Ridley once observed, if planning restrictions had been in force 500 years ago, Britain would now be deprived of its many beautiful little villages and towns. New houses do not have to be ugly and horrible – it depends how they are built.

Sadly, some of the prettiest parts of the countryside have already been defaced. You can't go five miles in any direction without coming on a beauty spot scarred by a caravan site. These mobile blots on the landscape – many of them fixed there permanently, probably without planning permission, as second homes – are usually sited to give the occupants a pleasing outlook. Unfortunately, they can be seen for miles around and destroy the view for everyone else. Farmers call it diversification, the rest of us call it abomination.

Then there's the unofficial encampments set up by "travellers" which spill their rubbish, old cars, stray dogs and illegal lorries around the place before moving on to the next lay-by or field. Everywhere you go, you discover rusting old caravans for illegal immigrant farm workers, bits of old railway wagons converted into sheds, piles of old boxes and domestic rubbish dumped for a fee. Many farm buildings are semi-dilapidated. Many public footpaths are deliberately made impassable by barbed wire and bulls.

The people who care most for the countryside are the middle class refugees from towns and cities, the weekenders and the seriously rich who dip in and out of their private estates by helicopter. Many of our rural areas are neglected and run-down, not nearly as green as they seem, polluted by pesticides and crying out for the love and attention they only get when people live there.

It is surely time to reconsider our national planning policies. Developments around venerable old towns should be abandoned because they ruin attractive settlements. Instead, why not create some new settlements in the countryside?

As our planners contemplate another round of over-development in our historic county towns, the real countryside escapes unscathed. Of course, there would be fury if we plonked more places like Telford or Redditch on the soft hills of Herefordshire or the flat lands of Norfolk. But what about smaller developments like the 2,500 homes and 6,000 people of Poundbury, Prince Charles's experimental village outside Dorchester? Poundbury has had its critics but with its mix of town houses, cottages, shops and light industry it is a conscious effort to recreate the communities of yesteryear. It may not be entirely successful but it's a great deal more successful than most other modern developments.

Contrast this with the Government's plans for Milton Keynes. Already a hideous, flat sprawl of new town, it is to be expanded, over the next few years, into a city twice the size of Birmingham. But, as Britain's population soars from 59 million to an estimated 71 million in the next 40 years, planners are starting to worry about where all the water will come from.

And they have hit on an answer which may dismay future residents of Milton Keynes – in the not-too-distant future, the town's new houses will be built with showers only. Baths will be banned. For the people of Milton Keynes, a long, deep, relaxing soak will be no more.

This was bound to happen. We're already suffering supply problems with gas and electricity which may become worse if winters get colder – especially now we more or less depend on the unpredictable Russian Government for most of our power supplies. Water is allegedly, despite irregular flooding, an even more limited resource yet we usually take for granted that it will always be in plentiful supply.

The British Association for the Advancement of Science says we have less water per person than Spain or Portugal. And as the number of people in a household shrinks, so the amount of water consumed per person rises – a single person uses 120 pints a day compared with 72 pints for each member of a household of six people. Demand for water will continue to grow as our civil servants (who have all the real planning power) concrete over this green and pleasant land at the rate of 653 new homes in the Green Belt every year in the West Midlands alone.

Green belt developments rose 60 per cent between 1996 and 2003 and will carry on increasing. Some people think the Green Belt should be untouchable – set in concrete, as it were. Under Gordon Brown, it will be. Civil servants trained at the Stalinist School of Central Planning believe they know best. You can imagine them with a map of the country plotting the advance of their housing estates like Panzer divisions.

The immediate tactic is to plonk no fewer than one and a half million new homes on the south east of England in the next decade. Already the London economy is the 27th largest in the world. It will grow ever faster while everywhere else shrivels. But how can the south east accommodate all these people? The true answer is that it cannot.

To add insult to injury, the cost of all this will be met by taxpayers throughout the country. As stealth taxes go, this has all the makings of being the most unfair, unreasonable and secret of the lot because it amounts to a £50 billion "London Tax" to be paid by all of us. That is the likely price for providing the infrastructure necessary to cater for all the new houses London and the South East will be getting in the next 15 years or so.

After all, you can't build 32,000 new houses a year in London alone without the need for roads, trains, buses, schools, hospitals and so on to service them. It will cost £7.5 billion just to deal with the sewage and £3 billion for flood prevention. Similar costs will apply in the rest of the country as well. But the difference is that there will be so many more houses in London and the South East than anywhere else.

Most regions are facing an increase of somewhere between 350,000 and 575,000 homes. But the building boom will concentrate on London and the South East. Kent County Council says the infrastructure cost for every 1,000 extra homes is £96 million. London and the South East will get at least twice as many homes as anywhere else – well over one million. So we will all have to pay through a London Tax running to almost £50 billion in 15 years. That's equal to a tax rise for everyone in Britain of 2.4p in the pound. Oh, and don't forget, everyone faces a similar increase just to pay the infrastructure costs for their own region – so Gordon Brown's housing boom will cost us almost 5p in the pound on income tax.

These astonishing costs don't include add-ons like the £1 billion Gordon Brown wants to spend subsidising mortgages for "essential workers" in London or the £8 billion he wants for low-cost housing.

The natives are getting restless. Keith Mitchell, chairman of the South East regional assembly, says: "If Government thinks we're bonkers to insist on investment in transport, schools, hospitals and parks to support new homes, then I have to say we're proud to be bonkers."

The emphasis on the South East is all wrong. London is a nice place to visit but you wouldn't want to live there. It's full and filthy. If they're short of nurses or teachers, Londoners should move to other places where house prices are more reasonable and public employees are not in such short supply. Gordon Brown wants to distort the economy by subsidising people who can't otherwise afford to live in London. As we pay the London Tax, it will drain skill, expertise and enterprise away from the rest of Britain.

Let London stew in its own foetid juices for a year or two. Gradually it would become less popular. It wouldn't attract all the biggest businesses, all the best jobs, all the public money. Instead, the rest of us would profit. For instance, at the moment the State spends ten times as much, per head, on public transport in London as it does in the West Midlands. If that subsidy were abandoned, there be no need to discuss congestion charges. We could have a decent system of public transport. Mr Brown wants to build 240,000 houses every year. By comparison, there are about 438,000 houses in the whole of the Black Country and about 390,000 in Birmingham. It's true that homes are now so expensive many young people can't afford to buy them. We should do something about it. But building more and more in the most expensive parts of the South East is not the way to calm house prices.

If Mr Brown really wants more affordable housing, he must build where land is cheaper. That means investing outside London. It means concentrating on "brown field" sites in places like the Black Country. As a nation, we can't afford to subsidise Londoners any longer. Mr Brown ought to be cutting the London Tax, not increasing it. Unfortunately he's a Scot so he doesn't understand how unfair his policies are on most of England.

10
The world's first superstate-by-stealth

i Welcome to rip-off city

Queuing for immigration at Brussels airport, we are divided into EU "Nationals" and Non-EU "Nationals". Which am I? I thought I was English, or British, or at the very least a subject of the Monarch of the United Kingdom of Great Britain and Northern Ireland. I am wrong. I have become an "EU National". That's why my passport says "European Union". Welcome to the bizarre world of the European Union, the world's first superstate-by-stealth.

"Divide and rule" is the Brussels bureaucracy's secret weapon.

The Spanish are falling out over plans to recognise Catalonia – capital Barcelona – as a separate country. In Belgium itself the locals are seriously debating a split between Flanders (pop. six million, capital Brussels, language Flemish) and Wallonia (pop. four million, capital Namur, language French). This couldn't happen if it were not for the "EU Nation". It gives the provinces and regions of Europe the opportunity to declare independence without actually having to go it alone. As the countries get smaller – think Wales, or Scotland, for instance – the over-arching superstate becomes much more powerful.

The attitude is: Let the Flemish, Catalonians and Scottish worry about folk dancing, dustbins and preserving dead languages; the EU bureaucracy will deal with Russia, China and the United States, decide on war and peace, raise taxes, impose laws, agree trade deals, help the Third World, save the environment. It's a slow process, but it is happening.

Meanwhile Brussels – capital of Europe – is rip-off city. I take a taxi from the airport to my hotel. It costs 25 euros. A colleague makes the same journey. It costs her 40 euros. Later, a group of us take two taxis back from a restaurant. The taxis leave together and arrive together. The first charges 15 euros, the second 7.70 euros. It's not surprising that everyone you meet complains about money. There's never enough because it's all spent on French farmers. In 2006, the EU had £72 billion to waste; £35.7 billion of it went to olive growers, sheep-burners and beef-banners. However, the alleged shortage of money for other projects doesn't stop the bureaucrats from interfering.

Did you know about "Basel II" for instance? No? Nor me. Apparently it is how Eurocrats refer to new rules they have imposed on banks lending to small businesses. The aim, apparently, is to stop banks going bankrupt. As a result, in future it will be much more expensive, time-consuming and difficult for a small business to borrow money. No doubt this will contribute to the EU's business insolvency record. In 2004, no fewer than 156,245 businesses went bust in the super-state. That compares with 21,298 in Eastern Europe, 35,185 in America and a mere 13,934 in Japan. Another triumph for the euro.

I ask a Eurocrat why it's so bad in Europe and my informant admits part of the problem is the time it takes big companies to pay their bills. Late payments kill cash flow and end up sinking small companies. So what's the EU doing about this terrible problem?

The good news, according to my man with the chequebook, is that the EU is issuing a directive aimed at making people pay their bills faster. "We know in many countries it's a key problem for small and medium-sized businesses," he says. The bad news, though, is that it seems the European Commission itself is one of the slowest payers in Europe. Our hero confesses: "The Commission is one of the worst payers. We always pay – but sometimes we pay too late and it's too late for a company. It's a shame." Shame indeed.

But indifference to public opinion is necessary in creating a super-state by stealth. I meet a senior EU finance official. He's not happy. I watch an interesting disagreement between the finance official and a British civil servant over the millions of pounds each year that disappear from the EU's funds and can't be accounted for. The official calls this "criminal fraud", blames Greece and Italy and thinks something should be done. The British civil servant calls it "irregularities", says it really doesn't matter and it's all just a fuss over nothing got up by the press.

My financial friend explains how the EU is busy muddying the waters.

We know that inefficient farmers (not all of them French) get over half of the EU's multi-billion-pound budget. In future, all that money will be hidden under three separate budget headings, which means it will be much harder to establish exactly how much money is spent on farm subsidies. It's a simple cheat. Or, as my chum puts it: "This is the EU shooting itself in the foot. Its PR is usually catastrophic but this is beyond belief." With one magic trick of sly accounting, the EU will hide the hideous truth about the fortune it wastes on inefficient farmers. My informant is too particular. He is looking at it from an insider's point of view where this sleight of hand will actually be seen. For the outsider, though, it will look as if farm subsidies have fallen dramatically and nobody – certainly no journalists – will bother to turn over the stones to reveal the truth.

Visit the lavish European Parliament building in Brussels – where MEPs go when they are not meeting at the other lavish European Parliament building in Strasbourg – and you realise what a gravy train the whole thing is. To stop MEPs skiving completely they only get paid if they turn up to at least half the meetings they are employed to attend. And they have to sign-in, in person. Even so, some of them only spend one night a week in Brussels before flying home again – or topping up their tans at their Spanish villas.

This is how we are governed.

Coming back to Birmingham Airport I was astonished to see how busy the flight from Brussels was. But I shouldn't have been. These days, the decisions that affect us are being made not just down the M1 but just across the North Sea. And most of the time, none of us even notices.

ii No, non, nr, nein, αριθ, não, nie, nej, niet – Yes in Brussels

Imagine the scene. Buckingham Palace. The Prime Minister is angrily biting his tongue while the Queen tells him how to run the country. She takes him to task for failing to consult the people – her people. He listens patiently but, according to observers, when the audience is over, the Prime Minister storms off in a fury vowing not to let her interfere in politics any longer.

Yet within a few days later he makes a public announcement which conforms witih what his Monarch has instructed. He does not let on that he's acting on Her Majesty's orders, obviously. But he is, nevertheless.

This is not piece of history from the era of Palmerston, Gladstone or Disraeli with Queen Victoria but an interview between our own dear Queen and then Prime Minister Tony Blair. Only a couple of days earlier the Queen had received a petition from no fewer than one million of her loyal subjects asking her to authorise a referendum on the Government's decision to sign a new European constitution.

Much moved by this spontaneous display of loyalty from her devoted subjects, the Queen raised the question at her weekly meeting with Mr Blair. He did not enjoy these encounters. Previous PMs have seen it as a chore, an ordeal or even an opportunity to discuss affairs of State with someone who is sympathetic but hasn't got an axe to grind. Tony, we are told, regarded these events as a waste of time and he only endured them because it was expected of him according to our own, unwritten but nevertheless valuable, constitution.

On this occasion, the Queen drew attention to the fact that quite a lot of people didn't want to hand over British sovereignty to a United States of Europe. Tony left his meeting in a right republican fury. But a couple of days later he announced we would be granted the privilege of a referendum on whether Britain should sign up to the constitution. It was quite a concession for the man who began his disastrous Premiership promising to be "at the heart of Europe".

At the time, British MEPs were promising to "deliver for Europe". They were offering "greater transparency", the EU would be "more democratic, bringing Europe's institutions closer to its citizens". The Constitution was "the realisation of the European dream". You may wonder whose European dream they were talking about, because it was almost impossible to find anyone in the country who seriously wanted the Government of Britain to be handed over to Brussels.

Yet if it had been left to Mr Blair and our MEPs, we would have signed up not only to the EU constitution but to the euro as well, without a referendum. There is an irony, therefore, in the idea that it may have been the Queen – the representative of those undemocratic, medieval, feudal times when "the people" never had a say in anything – who talked him into a plebiscite which, in the end, never had to take place anyway.

If we sign up to the constitution, there won't be a role for Britain's Monarchy any more because there wouldn't be a sovereign nation for her to reign over. So it was probably in her best interests that we rejected the whole idea. But then there's a double irony because if we had, we would be using our democratic right to vote to reinforce the position of that most undemocratic of institutions, the hereditary Monarchy.

This is not the kind of irony the European Parliament would readily comprehend. Its members claim a democratic mandate because some of us turn out for their elections every so often. And few European Socialists seem capable of understanding that an out-dated, feudal Monarchy could actually be more appealing, not to mention longer-lasting, than any President of a United States of Europe they manage to throw up.

Anyway, why worry? The European constitution was decisively rejected by the voters in Holland and France, forcing the EU's politicians to shelve the whole thing. Except, of course, that it is neither dead nor buried.

When the Eurocrats signed off the EU Constitution – before it was rejected by the Dutch and French – our MEPs threw a party to celebrate. Though the Parliament had no legal mandate to vote on a constitution, the MEPs spent £262,000 of our money on lavish food, champagne and decorations hailing the EU Constitution. Apparently £25,000 was spent on "thinkers" and "columnists" from countries holding referendums, and a further £70,000 taking 100 journalists to the event. The MEPs treated themselves to a laser display and an orchestra. They spent £2,500 on balloons.

Just another junket, maybe, but symbolic of the fact that within the halls of the EU, the constitution was regarded as something of huge symbolic as well as practical importance. There is no way the juggernaut will be deterred by something as trivial as the will of the people, even when the people are French.

It's back. Welcome to "Nightmare on Downing Street II – Return of the EU Constitution." Everyone thought it was dead and buried. An ex-parrot or, more likely, some vampire nailed down in the cellar of a haunted castle with a stake through its heart and a silver bullet in its head. We breathed a collective sigh of relief. We decided if the French, of all people, think a United States of Europe is a monstrous idea then surely the world is safe from totalitarian, unelected, bureaucratic dictatorship after all. Life went back to normal. All we had to worry about were issues like EU human rights laws and red tape designed to make life worse for the law-abiding, cushier for criminals and easy for illegal immigrants, centralised taxation and so on.

Yet the monster wasn't dead. In the dark and hidden corridors of power, something stirred. They were bolting the constitution back together again, giving it electric shocks on dark and stormy nights, bringing the thing back to life.

When the Constitution was rejected by the voters of Holland and France, the Eurocracy was sufficiently taken aback to call for a "period of reflection" while they decided what to do. That came to an end when the EU decided to mark the 50th anniversary of the Treaty of Rome, which first set up the Common Market in 1957, with a new "accord". This "set out Europe's values and ambitions" through a new Treaty.

German Chancellor Angela Merkel was clear: "We will tell people again and again, in an open way, that we need this Europe and for that we need the Constitution." Nothing changed. The will of the people is entirely irrelevant. The Constitution is back and, in the view of many of our European friends, if we don't like it, we can sling our hook.

As Jean-Claude Juncker, the Prime Minister of Luxembourg said: "It is absolutely possible that the EU will move forward without the British if they reject the Constitution." An editorial in *"Handelsblatt"*, the German equivalent of the *"Financial Times"*, said: "The British will have to be confronted in the end with the alternative of approving the Constitution or leaving the EU. And there's only very few people on the Eurosceptic island who want the latter." The then Europe Minister Geoff Hoon admitted Britain may "accept an overhaul of European Union institutions without putting the changes to a referendum".

Interestingly, Labour MP Gisela Stuart, is one of the few people who has not been brainwashed by the monster, even though she had a hand in creating the Constitution by sitting on the committee which drew it up. She insists: "The first thing the Government needs to do is to state categorically that the Constitution is finished. Like the parrot: dead, deceased and no more. The second is to make clear that in Britain any future treaty which deals with the political and institutional arrangements of the EU, whether or not it is called a Constitution, will be subject to a referendum: it is the only way that a government can ensure the consent of the people in this matter."

Yet Mr Hoon claimed: "Our people must see the European Union as a real engine of change in their lives. When they think about the environment, they must think Europe. Climate change. Think Europe. Tackling world poverty. Think Europe." He was doing the dirty work for Valery Giscard d'Estaing, the mad professor who created the monster. Giscard, the ex-French President who drew up the Constitution, insisted it was still alive long after his compatriots thought they'd killed it off. He wanted the French to vote on it again and again and again, if necessary, until they produced the answer he wanted. He said: "Manipulators tell you: 'We cannot vote again.' What is this joke? We have to vote again until the French see what the stakes are."

This is the danger with referendums and the reason why their critics say they are the tools of tyrants. If the proposer of an idea gets an answer he doesn't like, he can either ignore it or call a new referendum until, from his point of view, it comes out right. When he gets the answer he wants, that's the end of the matter. No turning back. No second chance. Nothing.

iii The silent scream

When the BBC is stuck for news, it invents competitions. In 2005, Radio 4's *"Today"* programme went for "the most powerful man or woman in Britain". It was supposed to challenge our pre-conceptions and give us all the chance to demonstrate who we really think is in charge. Sadly for the BBC it all went horribly wrong – the listeners decided the most powerful man in Britain was José Manuel Barroso.

Who? You may well ask.

José was President of the European Commission and, as such, the runaway winner of the poll. He easily outstripped rivals for the title such as media tycoon Rupert Murdoch, parliament, the British people or the head of the civil service, Sir Gus O'Donnell. Naturally, in a poll like this, Tony Blair, the former Prime Minister, only rated 7th place and the then Chancellor Gordon Brown scraped home in 9th behind the internet search engine Google.

The Europhiles at the BBC cannot have anticipated their listeners would land them with what was, in effect, a strong anti-EU protest vote. The success of José Manuel Barroso, the former Prime Minister of Portugal, can only be seen as yet another silent scream of protest from the people of Britain at the way this country's affairs have been handed over to the EU.

The BBC is notoriously in favour of the EU and has treated its sceptical listeners with contempt for years. It regularly fills the airwaves with Brussels-inspired propaganda and only token recognition of the fact that the alleged Union is deeply unpopular with the majority of people in England. When in the summer of 2007 the City of Birmingham Symphony Orchestra was celebrating the 150th anniversary of Sir Edward Elgar's birth with a concert during the proms season, the BBC not only failed to televise it but chose instead to broadcast a concert by the EU Youth Orchestra in which the young musicians were surrounded by displays of the European flag. The message could not have been clearer.

Mr Barroso's success was clearly a protest at the way the organisation he heads had hi-jacked this country's laws and constitution. It was recognition that we are no longer free to run our own affairs in our own way.

As well as a general loathing of the fact that we are obliged to accept EU laws on everything from the rate of VAT to the cutting capacity of our lawnmowers, the vote was a recognition of Tony Blair's failure to protect £1 billion a year of our European budget rebate. This was not the kind of message the BBC wished to hear. It has been insidiously propagandising in favour of our loss of sovereignty for decades. And it does not take kindly to people questioning its ingrained values – of which institutional Europhilia is one.

Its reaction to the vote was revealing. Instead of reporting on all the different ways the EU interferes in our national sovereignty and explaining why Mr Barroso was so important, it invited Labour Ministers onto the programme to rubbish the idea that he's really the most powerful man in Britain. Even after an overwhelming vote for Mr Barroso, the BBC was in denial. It would not follow up this small example of EU democracy with a series of reports exposing the corruption at the heart of Europe. It did what it always does in such cases – and sought to prove its own listeners don't know what they're talking about.

This small incident is enlightening – though in one of its eternal naval-gazing exercises the BBC did later conclude that it suffered from institutional Europhilia. There was no suggestion it would do anything about it.

Still, one organisation which did react to Tony Blair's surrender over Britain's rebate was the EU itself, which vowed never again to let the heads of Government get involved in public rows about money. Tony Blair's humiliation at the hands of French President Jacques Chirac was the final straw.

The Eurocracy has a cunning plan to avoid these disputes in future. It's called direct taxation. By 2013 it is quite likely there will be a direct EU tax imposed on air fares or petrol or both. And we will be one more step on the road to a European super-state. The Eurocrats don't want anybody to know about this yet. It is so controversial they will do their best to disguise their plans, deny their existence and pretend they aren't happening. But there's no doubt about it – the EU wants to impose one or more direct taxes on the people of Europe without having to negotiate for money with the various member countries.

Levying its own taxes is something the Brussels bureaucracy has always wanted to do. It has several advantages. It gives Brussels power over its own income. Instead of sitting around while politicians haggle about contributions and rebates, the bureaucracy can be reasonably certain that it will get its money again next year. Direct taxes allow the bureaucracy to increase (or decrease, though that will never happen) its income simply by raising taxes rather than going through long, convoluted and fraught negotiations. And, of course, it reinforces beyond doubt the European Union's status as an entity in its own right – as, indeed, a super-state.

This will all be dressed up in the clothes of protecting the environment, saving the world from global warming, reducing Europe's carbon footprint and all the other right-on, politically-correct claptrap which is so fashionable these days. But it is really a naked attempt by the EU to give itself more power.

On a visit to the EU in Brussels, I met a very senior finance official. His view was simple. The row over Britain's rebate, and Mr Blair's fatuous bid to renegotiate the common agricultural policy, forced the EU's hand. "The way is wide open now for direct EU taxation," he said. "No matter how much opposition there is politically in the UK, in practical terms Governments will be quite happy if it gets them off this awful hook. I foresee a gradual shift of resources from the member states directly on to EU taxation. Numerous dossiers have been sitting in cupboards all over the European Commission just waiting to come out and now is the time. I can almost guarantee that at least part of the EU budget after 2013 will be financed by direct taxes on some activity such as aircraft flights or petrol. It will have to be a tax on something which can't easily be identified with a nation state so it will have to be EU wide."

At the same time, the EU is creating a new system for businesses which will make companies all across Europe pay tax in the same way – not yet at the same rate but it's a start. And it has a vice-like grip on every country's freedom to change the rate of VAT which even President Chirac couldn't wriggle out of. He became the most despised man in France's many restaurants. In his election campaign he promised to cut the VAT on restaurant meals from 19.5 per cent to 5.5 per cent. The restaurateurs were complaining the lower rate applied to take-away meals at places like McDonalds and this was unfair competition. So Monsieur Chirac promised a tax cut. He discovered he could not deliver it because the EU would not let him. Under its rules, VAT rates can always go up – the EU takes a cut from everything raised this way – but they are not allowed to go down again. Ever.

There were frantic negotiations on the issue but the French were blocked from getting a deal by the Germans, Polish and Czechs, among others. Consternation in the Elysee Palace – after all, no French President wants to be unwelcome in the establishments for which his country is re-nowned. But a *petit* spat over VAT is as nothing compared with a Europe-wide tax on flights or fuel. That, though, may well be one of Tony Blair's lasting legacies.

Alongside the desire to centralise taxation, the EU is – perhaps even more perniciously – centralising law-making. According to the Eurosceptic lobbing organisation the Bruges Group, environmental law has become an area of criminal law under EU control. It reckons a whole range of other potentially "cross-border" crimes may also be subject to Euro-law not national law. They include: counterfeiting the euro, non cash fraud (credit cards etc), money laundering through banks, people trafficking, private sector corruption, computer hacking and marine pollution. Other areas of law may also be determined by the EU including fraud involving EU funding, intellectual property rights and racism and xenophobia. At the same time, the European Commission is trying to create a "European Civil Code" which would undermine national legislation in areas such as contract law, liability law, family law and security law.

It won't happen overnight because in Brussels these things never do. The European Union is used to biding its time and then striking. The Constitution so decisively rejected by, of all people, the French, has not disappeared. It is already returning.

11
Kicking and screaming into the 14th century

Suppose the tree-huggers and doom-mongers are right. Suppose Arnie Schwarzenneger and Tony Blair's accord over gas-guzzling cars does not solve global warming. Suppose the Bishop of London is under-stating his case when he declares that going on holiday by plane is a sin. Suppose economist Sir Richard Stern's plan for green taxes doesn't do the trick. Suppose the record July 2006 temperatures in Britain and around the world are not just freaks of nature but a sign of things to come. Suppose power cuts in Oxford Street, freak flash floods and an invasion of mosquitoes are just the harbingers of doom. Suppose the soakings of the summer of 2007 we not a once-in-a-hundred-years freak of nature.

Then what?

If the worst comes to the worst, the ice caps melt, Pacific islands are swamped, half the world is turned into parched and arid desert and the rest is supposed to accommodate the survivors. The eco-warriors want us to believe this is all about to be unleashed on a complacent world. "Don't say we didn't warn you," they will cry triumphantly as the waves of the encroaching tide swamp London. If they were right, if the world really is on the brink of global meltdown, a catastrophe at least as big as the one which did for the dinosaurs, what can we do about it?

There are those who say we should turn off our computers and stop using the internet because, contrary as it may seem, the servers needed to keep them running, and the air conditioning needed to keep them cool, con-sume vast rain forests of energy. Then again, we can't drive to work because we will blow a hole in the ozone layer. Indeed, we can't really use any electrical appliances at all. Nor should we be using more than the bare minimum of water because that's a natural resource which is drying up (unless it's flooding, of course). Indeed, if the doomsters are right, we should be heading rapidly back to the pre-Industrial Revolution days when the only transport was a horse and the only food was what you could grow or kill on your own doorstep.

They rub their hands together with glee and tell us not only that the climate's changing, but that it's all our fault; we must be punished and forced to pay for our crimes against humanity. We have been selfish for far too long – driving our gas-guzzling cars, using our central heating, flying away to foreign climes whenever we feel like it.

Sir Richard Stern's 2006 report was welcomed as the excuse everyone was looking for to introduce new taxes on motorists and tourists. He said we couldn't live like this any longer, we couldn't go on indulging ourselves at the expense of the planet, we couldn't mortgage the future for our children and our children's children. His doom-laden warnings were welcomed everywhere. It was Tony Blair's parting gift to a bewildered country – the most important report of his premiership, he claimed. Gordon Brown was given the perfect excuse for increasing taxes. Soon we won't be able to fly anywhere, drive anywhere or even keep warm around our single, energy-saving one-bar heaters. It's probably just as well since the Bishop of London, Richard Chartres, says taking cheap flights is a sin.

Oddly, little was made of the fact that the combined emissions of greenhouse gases from the United Kingdom represent just two per cent of the world total. Any reduction in emissions from the UK was academic compared with, for instance, the effect of felling the Amazonian rain forest or the emissions coming out of the growing economies of China and India.

Worse than the new "green" taxes every politician is now so keen on is the endless preaching we now endure from every holier-than-thou bishop, politician and environmentalist grinning with self-righteous delight whenever a chunk of ice slips into the Arctic.

Naturally Sir Richard's report was couched in the apocalyptic terms reserved for these occasions. If you were asked to consider the worst-case scenario, I suppose it's inevitable you end up writing documents which look like the basis for the script of another Hollywood disaster movie. Even so, suspicion sets in early when he admits: "No-one can predict the consequences of climate change with complete certainty; but we now know enough to understand the risks."

Having admitted this "uncertainty", the report goes on to tell us that one sixth of the world's population, mainly in India, China and South America, could be hit by drought. "Hundreds of millions" in Africa will probably starve to death. Millions more might die of "heat stress" while malaria and dengue fever are likely to see off another few million. Rising sea levels would overwhelm countries like Bangladesh and Vietnam, not to mention the Caribbean and Pacific islands. The world's great cities – Tokyo, New York, Cairo and London – are all likely to end up under water as well.

Bizarrely, in the face of all this doom and gloom, Stern thinks it's fairly cheap and easy to save the planet. Indeed, it might even be profitable. He seems to believe that the price of saving the planet is a mere one per cent of all the money the UK economy generates. Billions, maybe, but in the face of apocalypse now, a small price to pay, I think you would agree. All it means is the Government gets to make us pay more for our cars and our flights, our recycling and our council taxes.

Somehow this still doesn't seen to add up. Either there is a serious crisis which requires urgent and concerted action. Or there isn't.

If there is, then sticking another 10p on a gallon of petrol or 17.5 per cent VAT on Ryanair flights to Spain looks like a very feeble, ineffectual, meaningless response to a looming disaster. When half the world is dead, there's not much point in waking up the next morning and saying at least we did our bit by taking the train to Wales for our summer holidays instead of the plane to Majorca.

It's a lot easier to believe we may face a little extra expense and maybe a bit of discomfort rather than contemplate the end of the world. Yet it is impossible to reconcile the dire warnings of the doomsayers with the modest remedies proposed by the politicians and their stooges.

If there really is strong and irrefutable evidence that the climate is changing and that the dramatic shifts predicted by environmentalists will actually come about, then it requires a serious and sustained response by Governments around the world which will drag most of us kicking and screaming back to the 14th century. But if politicians tried to do that, who would vote for them? Even if some politician were foolish enough to adopt the green mantle entirely, what would be the point of Britain making the ultimate sacrifice to save the planet if no other country were willing to go along with it?

And yet every time there are flash floods in Shrewsbury or a deluge in North Yorkshire swamping homes and washing cars away, or the inundation of Warwickshire, Worcestershire and Gloucestershire, let alone of New Orleans, we are told global warming strikes again. The polar ice caps are melting, the ozone layer is depleted, the seas are swamping atolls and islands in the South Pacific; the next tsunami won't be a natural disaster but the fault of our own self-destructive greed....

The warnings go on and on. There are basking sharks in Scotland – that must be because the warmer seas have sent all the plankton north for the summer and out of the English Channel. A few beech trees are looking a little parched – that's because unusually low levels of rainfall mean the entire landscape of England is about to change for all time. There is another shortage of water in East Anglia – it's got nothing to do with a growing population and excessive, wasteful demand because there's a drought brought on by our addiction to greenhouse gases. These days global warming is blamed for every natural phenomenon. Anything unusual or unexplainable in any other way. Anything rare or special. Any natural or unnatural event in the natural world that's a record – colder, hotter, wetter, drier, more humid, longer, shorter, redder, whiter, browner, blacker.... It's all down to global warming.

And every time these things occur you can guarantee there will be a small army of frowning, concerned activists, scientists and what George Orwell called bearded fruit-juice drinkers with a vested interest in maintaining the story of doom and destruction. A generation ago, these same people, or their parents, were warning not of global warming but if an impending new ice age. In the '60s and '70s, the big freeze was the big draw for the environmentally right-on activist. Mind you, in those days tree-hugging was a minority pastime. The big issue for the doom-merchants was mutually-assured nuclear destruction. Naturally they got that one wrong which is why they're now into a whole new doomsday of our own making. Curiously the new ice age threat melted away in the hot blast of global warming, this generation's Big Issue.

We're all interested in the weather. We all like nature and gardens, trees and seas. None of us wants to harm the environment. So it's the easiest thing in the world to play on our fears and wind us up to believe that this time the end really is nigh (even though it wasn't over nuclear weapons or the ice age or God's wrath striking down poor miserable sinners etc etc). It is possible some climate change is taking place. It is equally plausible that some of these changes will be harmful. Some of this may be the result of man's activities. But it could be a natural, cyclical phenomenon. Who can really tell for certain? The prophets of doom tell us, for instance, that global warming means the end of the gulf stream and this country's climate will become colder and wetter; others insist we will endure water shortages while the vineyards of the Severn Valley will replace the arid deserts of the Loire. Nobody really knows.

Next time a scientist goes on the TV to explain why swallows are dying out, or why tornados are now commonplace, or why skin cancer deaths have risen, listen carefully. You will always hear the same point being made. They need more "funding" to carry out further research into their chosen phenomenon. They will be using their particular piece of scare-mongering as a special new reason why the taxpayers should be obliged to bung them more money. It happens all the time. Experts always demand more money. But if they stand to gain out of the latest scare we can't trust them to be fair, objective and rational. They play on our fears to build up their little empires.

And then, of course, there is America – the Great Satan. It's still legal to be racist about the Yanks. We can accuse them of every sin in the book but especially greed and selfishness. To eco-warriors, America is big, rich, powerful and stupid. It's people are self-indulgent and fat. Its

President is dumb and its politics in thrall to multi-national corporate giants and oil tycoons who run the world without a thought for the future of our precious planet. Global warming gives liberals everywhere the perfect excuse for hating Americans. But even that doesn't mean we're all doomed.

It is true there is a general agreement among most scientists that the world is warming and heading towards disaster. Yet a cursory investigation of the subject reveals there are many experts who disagree with this alleged consensus and argue that global warming is a myth. It is difficult not to conclude that global warming is one of those threats humanity invents to scare itself. Humankind has always imagined global catastrophe and this is just another example of that kind of thinking. There may be some change afoot but nobody is sure of the explanation – some say it's sunspots which have been heating up in recent years and will cool down again in due course.

Scientists say the globe will warm in the course of the 21st century by between 2.5 degrees Fahrenheit and 10.4 degrees Fahrenheit – a pretty wide range, it has to be said. They claim that if this would be the most dramatic temperature change in the past 10,000 years and would have catastrophic consequences.

Campaigning in Rowley Regis on bright April evening in 2007, I gazed out over the Stour valley towards the Clent Hills and enjoyed a magnificently clear, sharp view across the Black Country. It was difficult to believe this area was given its name because, 150 years ago, it was shrouded in smog all year round. Metal really was bashed in those days. Foundries and forges bellowed forth smoke and steam day in, day out. The place was a black bedlam.

Today there's scarcely a smoke-stack in sight, let alone a trail of smog other than the vapour trails of passing planes. It was much the same in other parts of Britain in the Coal Age. Clean Air Acts and improved technology – not to mention the export of manufacturing to the Far East – have changed all that. So why are we doing more harm to the environment now than we were in the Victorian era when fossil fuels fuelled an entire empire?

On May Day – a date deliberately chosen because mayday is the international distress signal – I was one of those summoned to the virtual presence of the Prince of Wales to be told how bad things were getting. Prince Charles was speaking by somewhat dodgy satellite link from St James's Palace to groups of people dotted around the country. There were about 100 of us at the Hippodrome Theatre in Birmingham.

I felt as if the Heir to the Throne was looking straight at me when he accused some of us of still being sceptical about the whole thing. We "enviro-sceptics" are like the frog dropped into luke-warm water, he said. We carry on swimming around quite merrily until the water reaches boiling point, when it's too late, we're frazzled and finally croak.

"If the scientific consensus is correct, and there really can be no doubt at all that it is, doing nothing is simply not an option," he told us. "I don't want my children or grand-children saying to me 'Why didn't you do something when it was possible to make a difference and when you knew what was happening?' We are doing it for those who come after us, that's why it really matters."

Then there was Sir Crispin Tickell, once Our Man at the UN and one of the first people to warn about climate change back in the 1970s. He went on about insects, melting ice caps, drowning cities, refugees trekking across arid deserts in search of water and all the rest of it. "The world should invest a small proportion of its resources to avoid boiling the planet," he said. "It's a threat worse than terrorism."

Of course there were the usual scary statistics: the world economy could shrink at 20 per cent a year if global warming isn't tackled; 11 of the past 12 years have been the hottest on record; 200 million people could become refugees from flood or drought. It's planet meltdown – yet there is apparently a way out. It means carbon trading schemes, higher taxes, low-carbon transport, congestion charges, carbon labelling on products.

Faced with all this, I thought I'd better see how much it was likely to cost me to cut my personal carbon footprint. So first of all I investigated how big that great big footprint was in the first place. It turns out some people think each of us is responsible for six tonnes of Carbon Dioxide emissions a year. Others claim it's 12 tonnes. According to www.carbonfootprint.dom it's five tonnes on average but, based on my profligate lifestyle, I'm guilty of seven tonnes all by myself.

Still not to worry. If I turn off the CD player and the TV instead of leaving them on stand-by, fit energy-efficient light-bulbs, turn the central heating down one degree and skip work twice a week, then I'm half way to saving the planet.

Then it starts to cost money.

All the big energy-savers cost – and it takes so long to get your money back the ice caps will have melted long before your investment brings in any financial return. For instance, you're supposed to chuck out all your old kitchen appliances and replace them with machines carrying the Energy Saving Recommended logo. I reckon a new fridge, freezer, dishwasher and washing machine would probably cost about £1,250. That would reduce our energy bills by £45 a year, taking 27 years to get our money back. Mind you, it's not that easy to get shot of an old fridge these days because they're terribly unfriendly to the environment, being chock full of ozone-depleting gases.

Never mind. We're also told to fit double glazing to the windows. The National Energy Foundation reckons it would save as much as £80 to £100 a year. Snag is it would cost about £400 a window to install, if you did eight at one time, making the cost £3,200. It may be mildly eco-friendly but it's not terribly bank manager-friendly.

Another wheeze is to spend £2,500 on a new condensing boiler for the central heating. This saves us £200 a year which means pay-back takes a mere 12 years or so. There are some more cost-effective measures: cavity wall insulation costs £400 and saves about £150 a year; loft insulation costs £250 and saves £200 a year; a jacket round the hot water tank costs £20 and saves about the same in a year. Even so, for an investment of £7,620 we would have to feel pretty pleased with ourselves. We won't get our money back in a hurry but at least we would be doing our bit to save the planet.

Alas that's not the end of it. To make a real difference we've got to start thinking about our travel plans as well. The car is an evil, dirty, filthy little machine, the spawn of Satan, and to be treated with contempt. Or at least it's to be left at home twice a week. That is easier said than done. Can you actually get to work on public transport whether you want to or not? Do you need a car during the course of your busy day? Can you cycle to the office instead? Or jog?

I tried abandoning the car and commuting by train or bus, for the benefit of a Channel 4 "Dispatches" programme. The car journey took 50 minutes, even in the rush-hour. It turned out that the train would only add about a half an hour each way to my travel time (excluding waiting around for it to arrive) while the bus increased the journey in and out of Birmingham by two hours. For many people, that dead time of one or even two hours extra every day is such a disincentive they will never give up the car in exchange for public transport. And any Government that's serious about trying to reduce the volume of traffic on our roads must first crack the real problem which is the lack of decent, reliable, swift and efficient public transport.

Maybe we must all become home-workers if we are to save the planet. Except then they'll be heating and lighting offices and factories for us while we're wasting more energy heating and lighting our own homes. Still, using the car is not entirely forbidden even if the Energy Savings Trust says 22 per cent of this country's CO_2 emissions are caused by road transport.

Apparently we should simply drive more carefully to conserve fuel. All we need to do is avoid idling the engine, make sure our tyres are properly inflated, select the right gear, use the air conditioner sparingly, use the cruise control and get the car regularly serviced. Oh and don't drive aggressively but do stick to the speed limits. It's all pretty easy, isn't it?

Tootle along at 28 mph smiling at everyone, smug in the knowledge that you, too, are a fully paid-up eco-warrior. And by missing two days at work we're saving lots of travel money – assuming we don't get sacked of course.

Then there is that other big issue – going on holiday. It's our holiday-making which really kills the planet, allegedly. According to the National Energy Foundation each of us is responsible for 116 kilogrammes of CO_2 emissions on a 400-mile flight. On that basis, a return trip to Spain might account for about half a tonne of CO_2 per passenger. Go by train and it would be worth just 10 kilos per hundred miles.

Somehow, though, I still don't believe saving the planet can be this simple. Who seriously thinks buying a new fridge, a few expensive light-bulbs and a wet week in Aberdovey will compensate for the filth chucked into the atmosphere by the People's Republic of China? Global warming may be an issue that affects us all – but it's not one that many of us can affect, no matter what the eco-preachers tell us.

Unfortunately, my reaction is still why should I bother buying "green" light-bulbs or travelling by bus when whatever contribution I make to reducing the amount of CO_2 in the atmosphere is more than offset by the increases spewing forth in India or China? According to Jonathon Porritt, the "guru of green", that's a totally unacceptable attitude. How can our Government persuade developing nations to cut their emissions if we're not setting an example? Even the appropriately-named Stephen Fry is in on the act. He says: "The future of the planet is in your hands in a way that's never been available before. All it takes is will."

Sitting at Prince Charles's conference, I kept thinking of the 365 economists who were all proved wrong when they wrote to "The Times" in 1981 claiming Margaret Thatcher was destroying the economy. I still don't understand why the Black Country today, with its clear views, should be responsible for more, and worse, pollution than it was a century and a half ago.

Obviously it makes sense to save money cutting fuel consumption. But will I really save the planet by using a cooler setting on my washing machine? It's difficult to remain an enviro-sceptic in the face of so many important and intelligent people telling you what dire straits we're in. I can't reconcile the claims that we can enjoy a good standard of living and economic growth yet still save the planet from climate change by a few modest amendments to our lifestyles. May be I'm being perverse but it sounds a bit too much like someone wanting to have his cake and heat it.

As global warming began with the industrial revolution and, in this country at least, was probably at its worst when we were spewing out coal smoke, you would assume the earth heated up dramatically in the 20th century, wouldn't you? Actually it increased by one degree Fahrenheit. Yet we are asked to believe it will be ten times as bad in the coming 100 years.

This, above all, is why politicians are happy to use it as an excuse for new taxes but do not have any intention of forcing us back into the Middle Ages. We must assume that it's because, fundamentally and despite all the concerns from so many people, they don't believe the propaganda either.

Yet having flown back from holiday in France to arrive home just as three feet six inches of water engulfed my house and 60,000 others in Warwickshire, Worcestershire and Gloucestershire in July 2007, I cannot deny my confidence in my disbelief in the reality of global warming and its effects on our world has been shaken. It was a hideous homecoming and not something I would wish on anyone.

If the reality is that in future we face being drowned in floods and fried by heatwaves then why don't we take it more seriously? Instead of laughing at the crusties who camp outside Heathrow Airport, we should be marching at their side. After all, if 'planes pollute as much as we are told and if global warming is as serious as everyone says – and if it really did cause my house to drown along with so many others – then the need to do something about it will not be helped by an extra runway at one of the world's busiest airports any more than a runway extension in Birmingham or any similar development will do anything but make the situation worse.

Of course, there's the argument that we will soon have cleaner 'planes. But against that is the proliferation of cheap flights. Can we rely on technology as our salvation? Maybe I would just prefer to bury my head in the sand. I do not want to give up my comfortable 21st century existence and I certainly will only go back to the 14th century kicking and screaming.

I have had cold water poured on my cynicism and scepticism leaving me, I must confess, floundering. The July 2007 flooding came a year after a nationwide heat-wave which was, we were told every day during the summer of 2006, the precursor of long, parched, waterless summers to come.

One year on, a great river swept across our back garden and into our house. The global warming experts say it was one of those "freak weather conditions" they had been warning about all along.

It was a pretty devastating experience. And as you rebuild your home from such an incident, it is inevitable you wonder again about the truth or otherwise of global warming. In the end, a good flooding leaves you none the wiser. Were we the victims of a one-in-150-years event or of global warming? Will it happen again very soon or not in my lifetime?

The environmentalists will say that, even if they're wrong, we can't possibly take the chance. They have a point. But if we accept the need to take action, I still do not believe getting an A-rated fridge freezer and paying a £10-per-flight summer holiday tax is anywhere close to an answer. The problem is that real solutions involve an entirely different lifestyle for all of us. And that's just too awkward to contemplate.

12
Human rights versus the war on terror

Those of a sensitive disposition please look away now. What you are about to read is not my opinion but someone else's. Though I am not saying I disagree with these sentiments, if I were to express them openly and in my own name, I would probably get arrested. I'd certainly be accused of right wing bigotry and extremism. This is the sort of thing you might only expect to hear in public down the pub at a BNP meeting. That's why these opinions are so interesting. Because the speaker is a successful Indian businessman who happens to be living in Birmingham for a while.

When I met him, and almost before we'd said hello, he was telling me what a terrible country it was and what a dreadful Government we were saddled with. To start with I thought he was talking about India but it soon became apparent he was talking about Brown's Britain

"This Government," he said. "It let's criminals get away with it. Immigration – so bad they're letting anybody in. All kinds of riff-raff. People who don't even speak English. Too many Asians, too many blacks, too many Moslems. I'm from India myself and I know. There was a time when Britain was respected around the world. The Empire was a great thing. Your country set the world an example. Your country knew about discipline, good behaviour, fair play and decency – the stiff upper lip. Now? Now your Government can't control anything. Guns sold in pubs for thirty pounds. Thirty pounds! It's mainly the immigrants. Asians, blacks, Moslems. Too many religions – too much trouble. Too much soft thinking. In India, a criminal gets knocked about a bit, everybody thinks it serves him right. He knows he might get injured, hurt. Nobody cares. He's a criminal. Not got many human rights. Here? Here the police are frightened to touch anyone – accused of harassment, racism, brutality. What about just doing their jobs? Why aren't the police allowed to protect the public in this country?"

He went on in this vein for some time before going on to boast about the growing strength of India's economy and lament the tribalism, caste system and religious fanaticism of his own countrymen.

It does us good sometimes to see ourselves as others see us. India was once "the Jewel in the Crown" of the British Empire. A nation rich in culture and resources which we exploited and developed for good and ill. Today it is becoming one of the world's industrial powerhouses – manufacturing industry in India enjoyed 13 per cent growth in 2006. When did British manufacturing last register anything remotely like that?

Here, though, we agonise about whether immigrants should be given interpreters or expected to learn English. We debate ad nauseam the question of whether we are truly multi-cultural, what the expression means anyway, and whether we want to be. We are almost too frightened even to pretend to notice the fact that gun crime is almost exclusively perpetrated by young, black men.

Instead, our leaders talk around the subject. After another spate of teenagers killing teenagers in south London, Tony Blair – who was partly responsible for the collapse of traditional family values – said we were not seeing the breakdown of society.

My Indian friend is not alone in the views he expresses. Racism, after all, is not a black and white issue and never has been. Ethnic groups around the world are often each other's throats – ask the Moslem civil warriors in Iraq. He is right to complain about the way we pussyfoot about these questions, refusing to ask really difficult ones or express truly "challenging" opinions. The politically correct armies have marched over freedom of speech. They have even trampled their jackboots over freedom of thought – a crime is a crime is a crime unless it's a racially-motivated crime in which case it carries double the prison sentence.

As a country we have talked ourselves into a corner in our desperate desire to be seen as liberal, open-minded and tolerant. It is now impossible to criticise the behaviour of any group of people, any ethnic minority or religion (except, obviously, the Church of England which is always fair fame) for fear of falling foul of the race relations police.

So it is left to people like my Indian businessman to speak for us. Because he's not white, he can perhaps get away with sentiments which, expressed by a pit-bull-owning, flag-of-St-George-displaying fat bloke with a pint of beer and a fag, might incur the full wrath of our PC police. Yet the fear of speaking our minds is a cause of huge resentment and bitterness which, in the long run, may well be more damaging than any hurtful expression of genuinely-held opinion.

The suppression of resentment and anger, especially among the dispossessed white working class, is why the British National Party will not disappear. It is easy for the liberal intelligentsia to dismiss the BNP as a bunch of right-wing racist thugs. I tend to do it myself (as in "a pit-bull-owning, flag-of-St-George-displaying fat bloke with a pint of beer and a fag"). But that doesn't mean the BNP will just go away.

In 2006, the egregious Margaret Hodge, one of Tony Blair's closest allies, said eight out of 10 white people in her east London constituency of Barking were threatening to vote for the BNP. They were once traditional Labour supporters angry at a lack of affordable housing – and blaming immigration, and Labour, for their problems.

"They can't get a home for their children, they see black and ethnic minority communities moving in and they are angry," said Mrs Hodge, then the employment minister. "When I knock on doors I say to people, 'are you tempted to vote BNP?' and many, many, many - eight out of 10 of the white families - say 'yes'. That's something we have never seen before, in all my years. Even when people voted BNP, they used to be ashamed to vote BNP. Now they are not."

Mrs Hodge said the pace of ethnic change in her area had frightened people. "What has happened in Barking and Dagenham is the most rapid transformation of a community we have ever witnessed. Nowhere else has changed so fast. When I arrived in 1994, it was a predominantly white, working class area. Now, go through the middle of Barking and you could be in Camden or Brixton. That is the key thing that has created

107

the environment the BNP has sought to exploit." Mrs Hodge claimed the anger is not down to racism. "It is a fear of change. It is gobsmacking change."

She also complained about a "lack of leadership" on race, and said the "political class", including Labour, was frightened of the issue. "The Labour Party hasn't talked to these people. This is a traditional Labour area but they are not used to engaging with us because all we do is put leaflets through doors. Part of the reason they switch to the BNP is they feel no one else is listening to them."

Mrs Hodge said white families were angry at the lack of housing since immigrants began arriving in the area, and because asylum seekers were being housed there by inner London councils.

"There was nowhere for the local people to move to and we did not re-invest in social housing, nor did the Tories. Neither of us have done enough of that. It isn't that we have done nothing. But where we haven't done enough is affordable housing for families and the quality of life for families. Were we to blame for the change? No, it happened on the back of Right To Buy. But we could have built more affordable housing. We must do that. It isn't happening yet."

She blamed inadequate action to clean up estates. "What we haven't significantly addressed are these issues that are the quality of life on council estates. It is the poorest whites who feel the greatest anger because there is no way out for them. It's an incredibly serious issue. It's the big issue. We need very much stronger leadership nationally to promote the benefits of the multi-cultural society. We have got to do it, the Labour leadership have got to do it. All the political parties have got to do it. I think if we are not careful and we don't respond and learn the lessons from Barking and Dagenham we could see that same fear of change trickle out elsewhere."

Mrs Hodge caused a sensation when she highlighted the issue. It was widely debated but nothing much was done to tackle the issue itself. Labour MPs set up a campaign group to counter the threat of the BNP.

But of course they were unable to address the real concerns of their constituents. A year later the BNP fielded no fewer than 750 candidates at the local elections. The party made no progress, winning and losing eight seats across the country. With a General Election vote of a mere 0.7 per cent it might be thought the BNP is a joke which counts for nothing.

But Mrs Hodge would not have highlighted the party if she was unconcerned. In the inner cities, the alienated white working class is looking for an outlet for its frustration. In 2007, the UK Independence Party was overtaken as the right-wing party of protest. In those areas where the BNP is active, it has been able to attract discontented voters who feel ignored by the other parties, as in West Yorkshire towns such as Dewsbury and Batley. Its influence on elections should not be under-estimated.

In the seven local government wards which make up the Parliamentary constituency of Halesowen and Rowley Regis, the BNP was the third most successful party at the 2007 local elections. The Labour Party won a third of the 24,808 votes cast, the Conservatives took 41.6 per cent. The Greens, the Liberal Democrats, the UK Independence Party and one or two others, achieved a combined total of 2,726 votes or 11 per cent. The BNP polled a total of 3,392 votes, a 13.6 per cent share of the votes cast. It's not the end of the world, or even all that telling. But it is a straw in the wind. And the difficulty is that the mainstream political parties have nothing much to say to the people who choose to vote BNP.

Margaret Hodge was right about Labour – a party which presided over an unprecedented influx of immigrants, legal and illegal, to the point where it was forced to admit it had absolutely no idea how many such people were now ensconced in Britain and where the liberal intelligentsia is on the point of throwing in the towel by declaring an amnesty for all illegal immigrants. Officially, 2.5 million people entered Britain legally between 2001 and 2006.

Can Cameron do any better? Well, he is pledged to withdraw from the European Convention on Human Rights. This move alone will make a difference. It should permit the courts to deport illegal immigrants who have committed a crime back to their own countries.

After bringing the convention into law, the Government discovered that, among other things, it was no longer allowed to deport alleged criminals – even terrorists. So it was forced to put in place various deals with regimes like Colonel Gadaffi's in Lybia which would somehow secure their human rights before they were sent back home to serve their sentences. These countries had to promise not to torture or ill-treat our deportees. Alas, the courts took the view that Lybia couldn't be trusted not to torture or abuse such criminals – as if anyone in Britain could care one way or the other.

So when two men accused of plotting to shoot down aircraft landing at Birmingham Airport faced deportation, Mr Justice Ouseley of the Special Immigration Appeals Commission refused to let them be deported and, instead, suggested they should be released from prison on bail. The judge said there remained a possibility that the European Convention on Human Rights could be breached if the two men were removed to Libya, although he indicated it was not a probable risk. "There is also real risk that the trial of the appellants would amount to a complete denial of a fair trial," he added.

The two men, who could not even be named in public, were found to be "a real risk to the national security of this country". One of them, known only as DD, was "a global jihadist with links to the Taliban and al Qaida". His brother-in-law Serhane Fakhet blew himself up in a raid by Spanish police in the wake of the 2003 Madrid train bombings. He was thought to be the ringleader of the terrorist group which perpetrated the atrocity. Another brother-in-law, Mustapha Maymouni, was jailed for 18 years in Morocco for his part in the Casablanca bombings which killed 45 people in May 2003. DD, who was born in 1975, was a member of the Libyan Islamic Fighting Group (LIFG), which seeks to replace the Gadaffi regime with a hard-line Islamic state. The organisation is banned in the UK. DD has used a number of aliases including Mullah Shakir Ghaznawi, Imad Al Libi, Hossein Abselam and Abdullah Bataebeid. Married to a Moroccan national, he arrived in Britain in January 2004 and claimed asylum. He has been in immigration detention since October 2005, five months after he won asylum in Britain on appeal – though how he managed to be granted asylum is baffling.

The second terrorist, AS, was ruled to be a "clear danger to national security – he is an Islamic extremist who has engaged actively and as a senior member with a terrorist group clearly engaged in support work for jihadist activities."

These men walked free because their human rights were deemed to be more important than their potential to murder and maim innocent men, women and children. And this is no isolated incident. It is typical of the muddled-thinking which has beset our immigration system for many years. Here are two men determined to bring down their own Government and any other which they happen to dislike. Yet first of all we give them asylum – presumably on the basis that they would be persecuted in their home country. Yet it is a bizarre immigration and asylum system which permits terrorists to seek refuge in this country from the forces of law and order in their own. Of course, there is a debate about the legitimacy of some of the regimes they may be fleeing. Col Gadaffi has not been much of a friend to the West over the years, though he's mellowed. But in the global war against Islamic fundamentalists it is simply unacceptable to discover that we have tied our own hands so tightly we can't even fight the war against terror in our own back-yard.

Faced with scandals like this, it is no wonder some people turn to parties like the BNP. It is not asking much to expect David Cameron to change the law to deport terrorists. And it's not as if the absurdities of our human rights laws are limited to making it difficult to tackle terrorism.

13

Asking for trouble

In April 2007 I was selected as the Conservative Party's prospective parliamentary candidate for Halesowen and Rowley Regis. I'd stood as the party's candidate in Birmingham Edgbaston in 2001 and lost. Most of my friends thought I'd got it out of my system. Plainly not.

The news was not universally welcomed even among people who one might suppose to be supporters. The web-site conservativehome announced my selection by warning that my pen would land me in trouble. It quoted an article I had written about Guantanamo Bay and subsequently placed on my blog. Under the headline "Spot the difference, Mr Blair", and with pictures of prisoners at Guantanamo Bay and the Royal Navy personnel seized by Iran, I wrote:

Along with joy and relief at the news the 15 British sailors are coming home after their capture at sea by the Iranians, we should be asking some serious questions. First of all, whose negligence allowed them to be taken prisoner in the first place?

They were taking part in a boring, routine anti-smuggling operation. They were supposedly guarded by a warship bristling with technology and a helicopter flying overhead. HMS Cornwall and its like are supposedly "the eyes and ears of the Royal Navy" so why was it fast asleep when the Iranian gunboats surrounded our boys and girl?

And why was the helicopter miles from the scene of the action at the precise moment when it was wanted most? Who was asleep on the job? Who is responsible? Why on earth to we support – morally as well as financially – our armed forces when they allow their own sailors to become victims of their crass incompetence and lack of preparedness?

Our sailors would never have fallen into Iranian hands if the Royal Navy had been alert to the risk – a risk we have experienced in the past – and taken basic precautions to prevent just such an ambush at sea. You could go back even further and ask why on earth our servicemen and women are obliged to behave as customs officers trying to cut off untaxed shipments of Honda car parts anyway?

Still, that raises another question – not why we are in Iraq at all (that's a question for Tony Blair alone) but can we really believe our own Government when it says the sailors were in Iraqi, not Iranian, waters?

After all, if our Government and our secret services were happy to lie to us about the biggest question of all – the justification for war – surely they are quite capable of lying about the location of inflatable dinghies in the Arabian Sea?

We now know, long after the event, that the war was not justified. Saddam Hussein did not possess any weapons of mass destruction. And even if he had, he could not have deployed them at 45 minutes' notice.

Those were claims made up by Tony Blair's liar-in-chief Alastair Campbell to justify a decision that had already been taken to go to war in Iraq as part of some perverse "war on terror" even though, at the time, Iraq was not a haven for terrorists. It is now, of course.

But that's entirely thanks to Mr Blair and President George Bush and the collective failure to have any clue at all about what to do with Iraq once it had been invaded. Meanwhile there is another question we must demand an answer to from our Government, our Prime Minister and our Foreign Secretary Margaret Beckett.

They rightly fulminated impotently about the violations perpetrated on our sailors by their Iranian captors. They complained about the way the sailors were paraded on the media, forced to make confessions, denied any representation, falsely imprisoned and so on. All these complaints are reasonable. But how can we reconcile our Government's outrage with its acquiescence – indeed its support – for the far more evil disregard of human rights that is Guantanamo Bay? The numbers change but in November 2006 there were still 435 people incarcerated there of whom 110 were due to be released and "more than 70" faced trial.

That leaves 250 or so detained without charge, without trial, without representation, without basic human rights, "at the President's pleasure". This is a sickening injustice which shames the entire western world and every Government which fails actively to oppose it.

Our sailors were forced to confess to being in Iranian waters whether or not they truly were. But why is that worse than, for instance, the confessions forced out of the "Tipton Three", who were held without charge at Guantanamo Bay for two years before being set free? Ruhal Ahmed, Asif Iqbal and Shafiq Rasul claim they were forced under torture to confess to taking part in a meeting with Osama Bin Laden even though they were in Tipton at the time.

No doubt most Guantanamo prisoners are terrorists. But if that's the case, prove it. Bring them to trial – in a reputable jurisdiction, not a kangaroo court set up and run by the US military. Charge them in public. Give them decent legal representation. Let the case against them – and the case for the defence – be heard. Let justice be done and let it be seen to be done. Justly, openly, fairly. Until we insist on an end to arbitrary imprisonment without trial of this kind we are no better than the Iranians who captured our sailors and detained them illegally, to the outrage of an entire nation.

You can't fight wars and pretend to support the self-appointed world policeman of the United States and retain any fig leaf of respectability if you behave with a complete lack of respect for the basic demands of legality and justice. Guantanamo Bay reduces every nation which connives in its existence to the same low level as the vile terrorists it purports to defend us from. It is a question of morality. If we are to claim any moral superiority, any rightness in what is done in our name, any sense of justification for our actions, it is essential that we uphold the highest standards of civilised behaviour. Fair trials, open trials, free and fair justice available to all – these are among the most basic demands. And we can't meet those demands.

So who is Tony Blair, who is Margaret Beckett, to complain about the Iranians? They are more guilty than the worst terrorist – more guilty because, unlike many a terrorist, they should know better.

This, as conservativehome predicted, did get me into trouble. Correspondents to the web-site queued up to attack me. "Gareth" said: "His blog may well cause him trouble. He combines glibness with a fondness for his own opinions which can only bode ill." "Umbrella man" said I was an idiot while Jennifer Wells (at least she left her name) said: "A would-be Tory MP should know a lot better. CCHQ should demand he closes his blog down before he gifts Labour something similar to that he gave Blair when he last stood."

"Doris" asked: "Is this man a complete joke? Often the police KNOW that someone is a habitual criminal but the evidence they have is inadmissable in court. The Americans KNOW that some (not all) of the detainees at Guantanamo are hard core terrorists who will try to kill hundreds of innocent men, women and children the moment they are released. The judgement as to whether our way of life is damaged more by releasing them (thereby risking mass murder) or detaining them (thereby compromising our legal standards) is a fine one. To mouth off that the US is at 'the same low level as the vile terrorists' is the kind of idiocy one would expect from a Pilger-esque leftist or a brainless shock jock. Which is Hastilow?"

Others thought I was trying to appease Moslems in my new constituency with my "anti-American blog", accused me of "silly dissent" and suggested I was one of "al-Qaeda's useful idiots". Another critic, "Jon W" said: "I imagine Sylvia Heal (Labour MP for Halesowen and Rowley Regis) is over the moon this evening. My experience of listening to him at a fundraiser a few years ago was unfortunately not at all good, his trenchant views are not the problem, it is the pugnacity of expression that

will leave many voters unimpressed with the quality of their candidate."
In fairness to myself, I should add that a few people wrote in support.
David Cooper said: "Nigel Hastilow's articles in the "*Express and Star*",
many (if not all) of which end up on his blog, generally show robust
common sense on issues that matter greatly to the over-taxed, over-
regulated and badly governed man in the street. There is scope for him
to become the Midlands' equivalent of Boris Johnson - no bad thing.
Here's to Tory victory in Halesowen & Rowley Regis."

"Richard" said: "He wrote a rather interesting book called *'The Last of
England'*" and while David Allen Green said he was "not impressed" by
the book, he did say: "I went to college in Halesowen and I also know
Rowley Regis very well. When Halesowen was coupled with Stourbridge it was one of the safest seats in the midlands. It is still a winnable
seat. If we can win this, we are making good headway with urban voters
again. Mr Hastilow is in the tradition of populist west midlands Tories,
both from the left and right of the party: Powell, Stokes, Beaumont-Dark,
Knight, Budgen, Blackburn, etc. For some reason such an approach is
appreciated locally, and so he will probably fare better than an A Lister.
I was not impressed by Mr Hastilow's book (I am sorry) but I am glad he
is emphasising the primacy of the rule of law in respect of those detained
at Guantanamo."

It is disconcerting when you find your failings discussed in public like
this, even if the conversation involved only a handful of people who
you've never knowingly met. It's one of the prices you pay if you stick
your head above the parapet.

I suppose "Gareth" will be in despair now my "glibness with a fondness
for his own opinions" has spawned another book, however unimpressive
it may be. And if you have bought this at a fundraiser I am sorry if my
"pugnacity of expression" left you, too, unimpressed.

But I do not apologise for my views on Guantanamo Bay nor do I
apologise for expressing opinions on issues of the day, no matter if they
are politically incorrect, inconvenient or, even, contrary to the party line.

Most people, not unreasonably, despise politicians (and aspiring politicians, and failed politicians). Glib and fond of my own opinions as I am, it would be more despicable if I were to abandon, at this late stage, the habit of independence of mind, and the determination to retain a freedom of expression, which have accompanied me – some might say dogged me – through most of my unimpressive career, in the hope of political preferment.

The aim of this book is to encourage debate and try to persuade the reader towards my point of view which is, I believe, the point of view shared by a many people in this country. It's also an attempt to address some of the issues David Cameron's Government will face when it comes to power. You are the judge of whether or not it succeeds.

I must add, though, that whatever the difficulties this country faces – from terrorism to global warming, immigration to the collapse of the health service – it is still a country to love, a country to be proud of and a country to cherish. That's why these issues matter so much, why you have read this far and why we have to do our best to conserve what's best about it in any way we can.

We can only do this if we manage to elect a Government which would scrap identity cards; put police on the beat rather than CCTV cameras everywhere; introduce firm immigration controls; protect the country from over-development; tackle the crisis in the NHS and in our schools; defend our sovereignty from the European super-state; and put best interests of this country first. That means we have to secure a Conservative Government led by David Cameron. It's our only hope.

14
Jack Straw's Chapter

"When the history of Gordon Brown's government comes to be written, this won't even rate a single paragraph." That was what Jack Straw, ex Foreign Secretary, then Secretary of State for Justice or some such, said on the Monday after the Saturday when Gordon Brown announced there would not, after all, be a snap General Election on November 1, 2007. Well this is a whole chapter. Admittedly the book isn't a history of the Brown Government but it would be dereliction of duty not to at least make an attempt to prove Mr Straw's prediction wrong.

Those who remember the party conference season of September and October 2007 will recall that it was completely dominated by a single, inescapable subject: the imminence of a General Election.

Gordon had become Prime Minister at a time when Labour was behind in the polls but almost immediately on taking office, the party's ratings soared. There were several reasons for this but one of the most signifi-cant was that Mr Brown was not Tony Blair. The sultan of sleaze had gone off to bring peace to the Middle East and spend more time with his memoirs to the universal relief of the United Kingdom. The result of this change was that anyone – anyone at all – would have been welcomed with open arms. The atmosphere was not dissimilar from the time when John Major took over from Mrs Thatcher, only more so.

The new Brown Government did everything in its power to distance itself from what had gone before. In particular, he and his Ministers let it be known that they would wind down Britain's involvement in Iraq as quickly as possible. They did everything they possibly could to pretend the invasion and occupation had nothing to do with any of them – not Jack Straw who was Foreign Secretary at the time, not Geoff "Buff" Hoon who was Defence Secretary, not even Brown himself, who was if nothing else the paymaster for the armed forces throughout the Blair years, responsible both for financing them and for leaving them short of the money needed for vital equipment like radios and guns that worked.

The arrival of Gordon Brown threw David Cameron, George Osborne and the Conservatives into disarray. They were guilty of under-estimating their man. They failed to recognise that anyone who can retain the role of Chancellor of the Exchequer and, in effect, Prime Minister of the UK while the official PM plays spin doctor and world statesman, has to have something about him other than a dour lack of humour and a desperate need to retain control of everything. Then, in the weeks before the coronation of Gordon, David Cameron and David Willetts, then the Shadow Education Secretary, scored a most spectacular own-goal.

Willetts, apparently because he was afraid his planned speech on education might not get noticed, decided to beef it up by launching an unprovoked and unnecessary attack on grammar schools. In the face of all the evidence to the contrary, this former pupil of King Edward's Grammar School in Birmingham announced that they did nothing for social mobility and the Conservatives were no longer in favour of them. As the announcement started rumblings of discontent among the grass-roots members of the party for whom the retention of grammar schools and, if at all possible, the reinstatement of more, is an article of faith, David Cameron proceeded to rub salt into the wounds. He declared that those in favour of grammar schools were "living in cloud-cuckoo land".

It was the start of the decline in Cameron's standing within and beyond his party. He later moved semi-sacked Willetts and climbed down to the extent that he promised to retain existing grammars. But the damage was done. Some people will never forgive him for what he did – not that Tories realistically expect a future Government to open a grammar school in every town (as previous election manifestos have promised) but because the row represented a significant turning point. It was, without Cameron intending it to be, his "Clause Four moment", similar to Tony Blair's decision to abandon Labour's commitment to public ownership. Yet in Cameron's case, unlike Blair's, it back-fired and provoked rumblings of discontent which lasted all summer. By the time of the party's Blackpool conference, clandestine meetings were taking place between discontented MPs and their party's wealthy backers with a view to getting rid of yet another leader.

Meanwhile Gordon Brown had enjoyed a glorious honeymoon. Taking over from Tony Blair he faced flooding, terrorist attack, foot and mouth disease, a credit crunch and a run on the Northern Rock bank and emerged from it all full of calm authority. He was seen as safe and secure, a constant in an ever-changing world. His poll ratings soared. By the end of August, Labour were 11 points ahead of the Conservatives and talk was starting to emerge of an early General Election.

Throughout September the debate and discussion of the possibility of an election was allowed to grow a life of its own. The media were not to blame for this. The Prime Minister, his Cabinet and his aides were given daily opportunities to dampen the ardour, to rein in the expectation, to limit the demand for an election. They singularly failed to do so.

By the time of the party conference season, every political statement or appearance by anyone of any consequence in any party was seen only in terms of its impact on the likelihood of the election and, then, the outcome of the election. Election fever gripped the conferences, the delegates and representatives, the politicians and the media.

Everything was pointing to an autumn election. The campaign co-ordinator was appointed even before Brown became Prime Minister. Work began on the manifesto within a fortnight of his accession. Jon Mendelsohn became General Election Director in August and Martin Salter, vice chairman of the party, announced: "I can confirm that the party has been put on alert for an early election that could take place as soon as this autumn." By early September, lobbyists and PR experts had been recruited and 30 new posts created including graphic designers, researchers, policy and press officers, a copy writer, direct mail officer and administrators. Donors and millionaires were lined up to cough up – Gordon's pal Lord Paul announced: "If there is an election and the money is wanted, whatever I can pay I will pay." The unions were pledging £26 million. Saatchi & Saatchi, which made its name promoting the Conservatives, became Labour's ad agency and issued a poster with a picture of Brown with the words: "Not flash, just Gordon".

The Prime Minister's advisers – Ed Balls, David Milliband and their ilk – were briefing anyone who would listen that the time was ripe. Balls even said on the BBC Radio 4 Today programme that delaying the election would be a bigger gamble than going early.

Leave was cancelled. Charity and quango workers were promised paid time off to rush to Labour's aid. Civil servants and ministerial advisers were ordered to clear their desks and look forward to a few weeks office. Local authority election offices throughout the country were desperately putting together plans for running the election (even though the electoral registers were out of date and the organisation at its low point in the electoral cycle). Mr Brown himself added to the fever by doing nothing to dampen the speculation.

And all the while the polls held out their seductive promise of electoral riches. By the end of the Labour Party conference, yougov, the polling organisation, was asking: "Why are the Conservatives doing so badly?" Their latest poll put Labour on 39 per cent and the Conservatives on 33.

The Conservative Party conference was billed as a disaster in the making. David Cameron had one chance to save his political career. The party was doomed to electoral oblivion. Neil Kinnock, whose mouth has run away with him disastrously on numerous occasions in the past, declared the time was ripe to "grind the bastards into the dust". The General Election of November 1, 2007, was done and dusted, won and lost, all over bar the voting.

George Osborne announced a clever plan to take all except millionaires out of inheritance tax. He also revealed plans to get rid of stamp duty for first-time buyers. And he explained how it could all be paid for with a modest £25,000 flat-rate, no-further-questions-asked tax on non-domiciled residents in the UK. This latter wheeze was a victimless tax, given that the people involved spend more than that avoiding tax already and would generally find the deal on offer by Osbourne a bit of a bargain.

Then Cameron himself spoke for 66 minutes without notes. He said little of significance except afterwards when, with his microphone left on, he hugged his wife, said "I love you babe" and "I'm knackered" but he was brave, forceful, strong and resolute and it won him many new admirers.

At the same time Brown went on a PR trip to Iraq. He announced the withdrawal of 1,000 troops as if it were new. In truth 500 were already opn their way home and 500 more hadn't even been sent to Iraq. This spin, and the blatant opportunism of visiting Iraq to steal the Tories' thunder was seen as a pre-election stunt and backfired badly.

The polls turned in Cameron's favour and against Gordon Brown. Dramatically. By the following weekend an 11-point Labour lead had come down to a three-point Conservative one in one paper and the parties were neck-and-neck in another. Either way, Gordon would not get a working majority never mind the ringing endorsement he'd been expecting. The Grand Old Duke of Kirkaldy was forced to march everyone back down the hill again, raise the white flag, surrender and pretend his decision to hang on for another two years or so had nothing to do with his being "frit" or bottling out and that he had always been against a rush to the polls.

That was probably true. A cautious and canny Scot, it always seemed incredible that he would risk throwing away his lifelong ambition on the basis of a few favourable polls. Yet Brown had allowed the speculation to run on and on. He'd let it domnate the conference saason and the news agenda. He had only himself to blame when he was left with egg all over his face.

The real issue – and the one which won't be resolved until he does finally call the election – is how muich damage this dithering did him. It was exacerbated by the fact that Chancellor Alastair Darling's subsequent Autumn Statement – clearly designed for the election-that-never-was – had been changed to include Labour's own bit to cut inheritance tax (itself a botched job offering a £600,000 threshold for couples. It meant little in reality because most people whose estates were worth more than that would anyway have made arrangements to use the £300,000 death duty allowance available to each on the death of the first spouse).

This debacle was, for Gordon Brown, as damaging to his credibility as Black Wednesday was for John Major. On that occasion his economic policy was shot to pieces when the pound was igniminously forced out of the European exchange rate mechanism. This time the Prime

Minister's personal standing was holed below the waterline – he was exposed as a spin-doctor, an opportunist and, wost of all, an indecisive ditherer. Overnight he stripped himself of his air of command and became another failed politician out for what he can get.

It's no wonder Jack Straw is unhappy with the idea of this chapter in the history of the Brown Government ever being written.

15
Change tomorrow today

Imagine if Gordon Brown does win the next General Election. The prospect conjures up such a bleak vision of the future: Even bigger Big Government, even more State interference; more decline and over-crowding; more spies on everything we do; more taxes and more regulation; more politically-correct rules and demands; and more bossiness and Gordon-knows-best intervention in every aspect of our lives.

Less freedom than ever before.

Freedom is, of course, a curious concept. We have never had, nor would we ever want, absolute freedom to do as we like without reference to anybody else. David Cameron is right to say there are some things that only the State can do properly – defence, for instance, or law and order. And we all rely on the state from time to time for a lifeline, a safety-net or at least a helping hand. But the more we depend on the State, the less we rely on ourselves and the more of our own freedom we give up.

What is this freedom? The freedom to do what? The answer is to live our lives according to our own lights, at our own pace, in our own way. Provided that we interfere or disadvantage others as little as possible, we should be permitted to do as we see fit. The other side of the coin is, of course, that we accept the burden of the responsibilities that requires of us ourselves, rather than turning to the Government in one of its many guises.

Freedom is having the opportunity to make your own choices without being told to go here, stay there, do this or don't do that. Especially not from some arm of the Government which is, after all, supposed to be our servant not our master. Freedom is earning your own living and being able to enjoy the benefits of your hard work without being obliged to give more than half of it back to the State through income taxes, National Insurance contributions, VAT, council tax and so on.

In almost any aspect of Government you can think of, there is a clear choice between freedom or the State. In education, parents must have much greater freedom to choose where to send their children to school. In caring for people, choice is again essential – the freedom to make informed and free decisions about where to be treated or cared for rather than the take-it-or-leave-it, one-size-fits-all approach of the State. Even in areas like law and order, the choice between freedom or the State is at the heart of the debate. Admittedly the freedom we deserve – freedom from crime – will mean the incarceration of criminals but at the moment the freedom is enjoyed by the law-breakers and that can't be right.

Gordon Brown, even more than Tony Blair, is a Big Government man. We know from his time at the Treasury that he wants to control everything personally. It's his instinctive response. Sometimes it works. In the crises of terrorism, flooding and foot and mouth disease which met him at the outset of his time in office he made a point of being in charge and being seen to be in charge. This was supposed to be reassuring and in some respects it may actually have been. But it clearly demonstrated his inability to delegate or give up any of the puppet strings. That may work for Mr Brown in the Cabinet but it also works for him in the country. He will not relinquish power to anybody. His every instinct is for centralisation and control as it is, of course, for his colleagues.

It should also be remembered that Gordon Brown is responsible for more or less everything that went before his elevation to Number Ten. As an alternative to Tony Blair, he was a welcome change. But Mr Brown was responsible for every aspect of Government during the Blair years except, arguably, foreign policy though even there he was still the paymaster and he who pays the piper calls the tune. Gordon Brown is responsible not just for 101 tax increases or his £5 billion-a-year robbery from pension funds. He's responsible for the waste and profligacy, the lower standards, the incompetence and negligence which have been the hall-marks of virtually every Government department since 1997.

From cuts in flood defence just before the worst flooding for 150 years to the failures of the equipment provided to our armed forces on active service; from the excessive generosity to GPs with whom you can't now make an appointment to our overcrowded jails and under-policed streets; from the failure to pay farmers or deal adequately with foot and mouth disease to the abandonment of an "integrated transport policy" – you name it, Gordon Brown is directly responsible for the chaos. Yet some-how he tries to pretend it was someone else's fault, not his.

This was seen nowhere more obviously than in discussions about the war in Iraq. Mr Brown pretended the invasion, and every aspect of the debacle, was Tony Blair's responsibility alone. Had this been true and had he been a man of honour or principle Mr Brown would, of course, have followed the example of his fellow Scot, Robin Cook, and resigned. He didn't do so because he was in the thick of it all along. Just as his every pronouncement and public spending pledge was unveiled half a dozen times, each time as if it were the first time, so his Prime Minister-ship has been characterised by a new form of spin – Macavity or Shaggy, call him what you will, when there's responsibility to be shouldered or a buck to stop somewhere, Gordon Brown will not be there, like TS Eliot's cat, or he will be announcing, like the pop singer, that "it wasn't me".

When the next election comes it will offer a clear choice – between freedom and State control. A Cameron Government will, above all things, let people live their lives as they see fit. It will ask for responsibil-ity but it will give freedom. A Brown Government will seek to rule every aspect of our lives.

We can be sure of what we will face if Gordon Brown and his crew are returned to Number Ten. The arrogance of power. The indifference to traditional minorities like farmers or small businessmen. The ever-ex-panding State with its insatiable demands on us for money, for subservi-ence and for toeing the politically-correct line at all times. It will be an England where police officers are social workers; where the armed forces are sent into battle with guns that don't work; where the economy depends entirely on State handouts to function at all; a country subject to the Colonial rule of the Scots and the European Union.

It is a dismal prospect. Tomorrow's England is with us today – but we still have a chance to change the future. For the sake of ourselves, our children and our country, we have to take it.

Welcome to my nightmare

It is mid-afternoon on Saturday, November 3, 2007. At this very moment, the preceding pages of this book are coming off the press. It is almost a finished product, just waiting the production of the covers. The book is to be used as a fund-raising initiative in support of the Conservative Party.

In the fine old English country town of Stow-on-the-Wold, my wife, my sister, my brother-in-law and I have just had a very pleasant lunch and we're mooching around the shops. My mobile phone rings. It's Mary Docker, the chairman of the Halesowen and Rowley Regis Conservative Association. She sounds surprisingly animated as she tells me she's had "The Observer" on the phone asking if she still supports me as their Parliamentary candidate despite my article in the previous day's Wolver-hampton "Express and Star".

She said she had every confidence in me and could see nothing wrong with the article. I laughed and thanked her. I wondered why she had rung me, thinking she must have been approached by some little local weekly paper because I could not imagine anything controversial in my "Express and Star" article. It was only when she made it clear she was talking about the national Sunday newspaper which belongs to the Scott Trust, owners of the left-wing daily paper "The Guardian," that a wave of apprehension rushed through me.

I began to worry. Why on earth should "The Observer" be interested in my weekly "Express and Star" column? It mentioned Enoch Powell but it didn't say anything racist. What was the problem?

I felt like I was about to take an exam I was bound to fail because I hadn't done any revision, or how I might have felt at a crucial job interview. I was jittery, short of breath, full of nerves. My appetite disappeared and my stomach started to churn. I felt physically sick.

By the time we got home, the duty Conservative Party press officer, Caroline Preston, had called telling me to talk to a reporter from "The Observer". She e-mailed me the line to take. She said: "The points to make are: You were not saying that Enoch Powell was right (then try and steer off any other questions about Enoch Powell). However – immigration is out of control and is putting pressure on public services. This is not a race issue. The Political Editor of 'The Observer' is Nick Watt – his number is 07919 014392."

I thought I kept to that line. I said what I had written in the paper was entirely in line with party policy as outlined by David Cameron earlier that week. The reporter pressed me on whether I had written "Enoch Powell was right". I had so there didn't seem to be much to "admit". Even so, that was the nub of the story – "Tory racist insists 'Enoch was right'".

Caroline Spelman, the party chairman, rang me shortly afterwards from a fireworks party. I could hear the whizzes and bangs in the background. She sounded exasperated and was telling me this was turning into a serious problem. She wanted to know more about what I had to say for myself. I said more or less the same as I'd told the newspaper reporter but by now it was pretty clear I was in trouble. Big trouble.

That night we attended a bonfire party at a friend's house. It was a pleasant enough evening but the jollity was interrupted by a second, longer phone call from Caroline telling me: "Your political career, your whole political future, is on the line here."

She summoned me to meet her the following day. We spent some time making the practical arrangements for our meeting, which was scheduled for 2pm at her home in the leafiest suburb of her Meriden constituency. She implied that this would not be a career-ending moment.

It seems the party's inept press office had been panicked into the sort of response that actually adds fuel to the fire. It announced to "The Observer" and then the BBC that I had been summoned to appear before the party chairman to explain myself. Had they merely dismissed it as a non-story, which they could and should have done, nothing more would have been heard of it. After all, in the first instance the idea that some obscure Parliamentary candidate had written an article in a newspaper mentioning the name Enoch Powell (who was, after all, a local MP) is not exactly news. Or at least it didn't seem to me to be news.

How wrong can you be?

The article itself was much debated over the coming days but, of course, little read. It said:

The woman on the doorstep speaks in sorrow, not anger. Her daughter has split up from her husband and is now a single parent with two young children. They all live with granny because the daughter and her kids have been refused a council house.

And, according to granny, that's because all the available accommodation has gone to immigrants.

The house is full. Granny looks a bit worn down by her new lodgers. The novelty of having the little ones to stay is clearly wearing off.

The family seems resigned to the fact that nobody will do anything to help. They have more or less given up complaining about the way we roll out the red carpet for foreigners while leaving the locals to fend for themselves.

When you ask most people in the Black Country what the single biggest problem facing the country is, most people say immigration. Many insist: "Enoch Powell was right".

Enoch, once MP for Wolverhampton South West, was sacked from the Conservative front bench and marginalised politically for his 1968 "rivers of blood" speech warning that uncontrolled immigration would change our country irrevocably.

He was right. It has changed dramatically. But his speech was political suicide. Enoch's successors in Parliament are desperate to avoid ever mentioning the issue. It's too controversial and far too dangerous.

Nobody wants to be labelled a racist. Immigration is the issue that dare not speak its name in public.

Yet everywhere you go, you hear the same story. There are simply too many people competing for the space, houses, benefits, public services and jobs this country has to offer. It's claimed we couldn't survive without immigrants to work in our hotels, pubs and restaurants, to pick our fruit and clean our hospitals.

But that's because we make life too easy for the five million or more people who could be working but enjoy life too much living off the state. Why are 1.65 million people unemployed when it seems as if there's a job for more or less anyone who wants one? Why are 2.4 million people claiming incapacity benefit when society is getting healthier?

In the past some of them would have been accused of "swinging the lead", "skiving", "scrounging" or "cheating". Now we're told they need "up-skilling" and then they would be only too happy to work (but for their bad backs). We only need so many Polish waitresses because so many people who were born and bred in Britain can't be bothered to work.

This week we have seen a slight but important shift. Immigration has come out of the closet. Even David Cameron, the most liberal Conservative leader for decades, has decided it's safe to discuss immigration openly. This is not about race; it's about numbers. I have been lectured on this, on separate occasions, by several Asian Britons. They argue that their families came to this country to work hard, get on, pay their taxes, earn a living.

Today, far too many immigrants – they tell me – wheedle their way into Britain in order to benefit from the generosity of our welfare state. Asian Britons resent this as much as anyone. And no wonder. Does anybody in the country really want to see our population grow by almost half a million every year so that in 24 years' time it will have increased by almost 11 million?

Do we really want to see the country devastated by another three million houses or more over the next 12 years? Up to two thirds of these houses are only needed to cater for immigrants. How on earth can we afford to meet other costs – council housing, roads, hospitals and schools – linked to this staggering increase in the population?

Do we really want increased taxes to meet the increased costs of an increasing population? We must police our borders. Deport without debate bogus asylum-seekers and illegal immigrants. Abandon the "human rights" merry-go-round.
Tell the EU we won't take anyone from Bulgaria or Romania or any other country which wants to "join Europe". And get rid of the 11,000 foreigners in our jails.

Alas, the Government hasn't got a clue how many people it's let in already. Home Secretary Jacqui Smith, the MP for Redditch, humiliatingly apologised this week after claiming 800,000 migrant workers had come to Britain since 1997. Turns out the real figure is 1.1 million. First we're told immigrants took 30 per cent of the 2.7 million jobs created in the past decade. Then the official figure was increased to 40 per cent. Now it's 52 per cent – making Gordon Brown's promise of "British jobs for British workers" look pretty silly. It's all guesswork. And the Government has even less of a clue how many illegal immigrants there are.

Of course it's right that we share the international burden of caring for genuine refugees fleeing persecution and death. But we're being exploited. Britain is seen around the world as a soft touch. We must remember that, as the grandmother I was talking to the other day pointed out, charity begins at home.

In retrospect, those comments about what happens if you mention Enoch Powell's name should have warned me. Anyway, after a night with virtually no sleep, I was checking the internet by 4am to discover the story had made the front page of "The Observer", the second most important item in the paper after chaos in Pakistan. The BBC website had picked it up and the corporation's radio and TV stations would be running with it for the rest of the day.

It was a bad morning. We visited our house, which was being rebuilt from the summer floods; took the dog for a walk; bought the Sunday papers; had a cup of coffee. A friend called to tell me the egregious Cabinet Minister Peter Hain, when offered an open goal by the BBC's Andrew Marr, delighted in declaring that I had "exposed the racist under-belly of the Conservative Party". It was at this point I knew pretty much for certain that I was a goner.

I checked my e-mails. Already they were flooding in. By the time I left home to visit Caroline Spelman, I had printed out 14 A4 pages of e-mails I'd received, all offering me their support. I had been sitting at my PC getting increasingly glum. But then I checked my e-mails and was overwhelmed by the sheer numbers coming out in support of me. It was stunning.

There was one – just once – which took a contrary view. It said: "Remove yourself as a candidate. You are an embarrassment to your party and your country." It is curious how, at such times, the insults somehow stick when all the praise and support pass you by. But actually I couldn't believe how much interest this story seemed to have provoked. Just as I didn't regard it as much of a story in the first place, I didn't realise it would create such a stir. It was something I could use to steel myself for the meeting with Caroline Spelman.

I got to her home early and parked in a gateway for a while listening to music and trying to relax. Her home is a big fortress-like late Victorian property which was probably built by a successful Brummie metal-basher. At five to two, I drove up the drive, rang the front door bell and waited. No response. I kept trying the bell, then bashed the big front door to no avail. Nothing. Eventually I had to call her mobile number and say: "Caroline, it's Nigel Hastilow. I think I am outside your front door but I can't make myself heard." In my mind I was expecting what I facetiously described to myself as "political re-education". Actually, it was worse than that.

Caroline took me into her kitchen and made us coffee. As she did so, she said she had been fighting my corner the previous evening and that morning. She said she had no wish to lose me as a candidate; that I was able and had a future in politics. She said others in the Shadow Cabinet were not so happy about keeping me on under any circumstances. She made me feel guilty for ruining her weekend.

She explained how sensitive the immigration issue was and how dangerous it was for the party to be considered racist. She said David Cameron had raised the issue on the Monday in such a way as to escape the accusation of racism. Then on the Tuesday, the Government had announced yet another cock-up over its immigration figures followed on Wednesday by Trevor Phillips, chairman of the Equality and Human Rights Commission, praising Dave for his statesmanlike reflections and supporting the call for a grown-up debate. Nigel Hastilow had managed, in one ill-considered outburst in a local paper, to undermine all that good work by raising the single name of Enoch Powell. She agreed there was nothing objectionable about the words themselves. She said it was just very unfortunate timing. Any other week, she said, nobody would have noticed, nobody would have minded. An experienced journalist like me must have realised the risk involved in evoking the name Enoch Powell. The Tories strived so hard to avoid being called the "Nasty Party" any more and raising the spectre of "Rivers of Blood" was really too much.

I explained I had not written about race, but about numbers; that immigration was a problem because Britain could not accommodate more and more people from overseas. I said it was all very well the party wanting to cut inheritance tax, for instance, but that meant absolutely nothing to the majority of people in Halesowen and Rowley Regis where the average price for a detached house is about £340,000. I supported tax cuts but would far rather the party had policies which meant something to the people we needed to win back if we were to succeed at the next General Election – the people in marginals like Halesowen (Labour majority, 4,300; swing required, five per cent).

We started having a debate about Enoch Powell and whether the mere mention of his name was racist and therefore beyond the pale. She talked of the "Rivers of Blood". I said what about the blood that had been shed by terrorists in this country, especially the London underground bombings of July 7, 2005, when four radical Islamic suicide bombers killed 52 commuters and injured another 700?

She said she had some sympathy for what I had written. She had immigrants in the Chelmsley Wood area of her constituency and it wasn't always easy for the locals. I said one of the problems was resentment that immigrants got council houses ahead of the local residents. She categorically denied that this happened.

I said there was a tower block in Halesowen with a number of flats specifically reserved for immigrants and therefore denied to local people on the long council house waiting list. She said that must mean we had a dispersal centre in the constituency – in other words, she admitted that what she had just said was untrue was, actually, true.

We soon realised this could go on for ever and get us nowhere. Caroline, a little apologetically, cut to the chase. My political career would survive if I signed a press release drawn up by Andy Coulson, the party's chief spin doctor.

Coulson is hardly the man for a crisis. Paid a reputed £485,000, he is the ex-Editor of the "News of the World" who was forced to resign in the wake of the phone-tapping scandal after his royal editor, Clive Goodman, was jailed for conspiracy to intercept messages to senior members of the royal family, and their servants.

Caroline presented me with the statement Coulson had written, which was to be issued in my name if I wanted to be kept on as a parliamentary candidate. It had been cleared by David Cameron and Steve Hilton, his closest aide. In his e-mail to Caroline, Coulson said:

"Hi Caroline – David and Steve have cleared the following. I've also given a guide for your comment which should be attached to any statement. Obviously you may want to change that. David feels strongly that the Hastilow statement is not for negotiation and once he has agreed I will brief that this is his final warning. If we could also get an agreement from him to avoid all media requests but clarify his position in the next (cleared) article that would be great. Hope all that's ok. Thanks. Andy."

The statement itself was to have read:

"Nigel Hastilow said: 'Although I did not – and do not – support Enoch Powell's 'Rivers of Blood' comments I accept that some of the wording of my column was incredibly stupid. Immigration is a valid and critical issue for all politicians and candidates to discuss. But the language we use and the references we make must be responsible at all times. David Cameron last week made clear that immigration is not a race issue and I fully support his and the party's position on this matter. I apologise for any upset my article may have caused.'"

Caroline would have added, according to Coulson's press release: "Mr Hastilow has apologised for his error and assured us that he will in future take more care with the language he uses on this issue. This was a stupid mistake and he accepts as a candidate he must be more responsible."

I read it all quickly and immediately decided I couldn't accept it, especially as Caroline then went on to say that I would be required to submit any future articles for the "Express & Star" (or anywhere else) to Conservative campaign headquarters for political correction before submitting them to the editor. It was this, even more than the "incredibly stupid" line, which I couldn't stomach.

If I agreed to the statement and the strings attached, I could have stayed on as the candidate for Halesowen and Rowley Regis. It was a temptation. You don't lightly throw away all those years working for the party and an opportunity to become an MP. But I felt that if I were to agree to these demands I would lose not just my honour and integrity but my credibility as both a journalist and politician.

It would have been such a climb-down. I would forever be seen as the grovelling "incredibly stupid" candidate who backed down to save his own skin. Even if I'd wanted to, the fact is that my previous book, "The Last of England," contains similar references to Enoch Powell in the context of the population boom. Though the book is hard to come by, it would not be impossible for "The Observer" to track one down and expose the fact that I had "form" where Enoch Powell was concerned.

Any respite would probably only have been temporary. I told Caroline I could not guarantee there would be no repetition in the future. I could not trust myself to toe the party line when my own strong feelings pulled me in another direction. This may mean I was never going to enjoy political success. But having given up the Editor's job at "The Birmingham Post" to try my hand at politics, having stood and lost in 2001 and having managed to get a second – and, given my age of 51, last – chance to become an MP, preparing myself to reject the offer was not something I did lightly. Indeed, at one point, the whole experience became so over-whelming that I felt tears welling up in my eyes and my chin begin to wobble. I had to march up and down the corridor biting my lip until I could regain control of my emotions.

In the end, though, I did not think I had written anything terrible or even off-message. I was not prepared to submit my future writing to the censorship of the party Thought Police and I would not be prepared to say I was "incredibly stupid".

I rejected the offer and started hand-writing a statement of resignation. It said: "I am very sorry that any remarks of mine have undermined the progress David Cameron has made on the issue of immigration, as on so many other issues. I have been here once before when William Hague was party leader and I have no wish to go there again. So, with regret and my continuing support for the future, I hereby tender my resignation as parliamentary candidate for Halesowen and Rowley Regis. I thank my friends in the constituency association for their support."

The mention of William Hague relates to the time in 2001 when a previous article of mine was taken completely out of context by Tony Blair and turned into a stick to beat the then Tory leader with during a Question Time clash. I shall not go into the details here but it is fair to say that was a cross I'd been bearing ever since. This time round it was even worse. I couldn't imagine how awful a third disaster might be and did not trust myself enough to be sure I could avoid such a risk.

Caroline had to send a copy of this statement to Coulson. She is, apparently, dyslexic so I was obliged to sit at her PC in her study on the third floor of the Spelman mansion and type my own resignation statement into her Outlook e-mail system and send it to the man who was demanding my head. I didn't mind. I wanted to oblige. I like Caroline. We're the same age. She was kind to me when I was first adopted as a PPC in Edgbaston in 2000. Now she was my executioner. In the olden days, the victim tipped the executioner. I gave her a goodbye kiss.

It seems as if people were not expecting me to resign. There was an element of surprise in the immediate news reports. Caroline whizzed back to London to announce that I had behaved very honourably. I met my wife and some friends, Tom and Jenny, and went to play tennis. It seemed the right thing to do. When your world is collapsing around you, do something normal. It was a cold, dark afternoon. Jenny and I won.

Later, I did a Radio 5 interview against my better judgment and only because I knew the producer a little. I had avoided most other interview requests and didn't really want to talk to anyone. What little I had to say beyond the official statement I had given to a friend who was a freelance journalist. He passed on to various papers the quote that said: "I could have stayed on but they wanted me to say sorry for something I am not sorry about. They made me an offer I couldn't accept."

On Five Live, I was cornered by a very aggressive interviewer who accused me of racism and asked if I agreed with the "rivers of blood" bit of Powell's speech. I said something about the 7/7 underground bombings but tried to avoid going any further down that road as it was in danger of confusing the arguments about population numbers with those relating to race. I was determined to avoid discussing race if at all possible because that was not, and never had been, my point – although it may have been others'.

I couldn't eat or even drink. Instead I wrote an article for the "Express and Star" recounting the events of the last 24 hours. I went to bed but didn't sleep.

It's very strange to know that every radio and TV station in the country is bandying your name about. It's odd to find every paper speculating about you. It's downright disturbing to find yourself branded a racist, a betrayer of your own political party and at the same time to be condemned for naivety. For 24 hours, it seemed as if I was the only item on the news agenda. On the Monday, everyone wanted to talk to me – the various different bits of the BBC; Sky News; Channel 4; the "Halesowen News"; everyone.

I spoke to the "News" and that was about it.

I was too busy trying to work at the day job and handle the vast number of e-mails I was getting. There really were hundreds. At one point I opened my Tiscali account to discover 451 un-read e-mails. I spent half an hour dutifully ploughing through them. They were almost without exception supportive. So much so, indeed, that it made the nightmare of the past 24 hours seem almost glorious – an heroic stand against the party machine and the politically-correct establishment. But when I had to stop reading the e-mails, I discovered the number still un-opened had actually risen to 460 – they were arriving faster than I could read them.

Those which arrived via my web-site nigelhastilow.co.uk were so numerous the system seized up and I couldn't reply to any of them. Others came via my work e-mail address or were forwarded from the Dudley Conservative Party office in Halesowen. The tenor of these e-mails was similar to the earlier messages, only now there was the additional outrage generated by my resignation.

These e-mails made such a difference. As a journalist in one capacity or another most of my working life, I was accustomed to stimulating a bit of controversy. I always believed it was a good thing to do. Debate and argument are the essence of a good newspaper and that was often what I tried to create both as an editor and as a politician. That is why newspapers employ opinionated columnists.

At the "Express and Star," one measure of success is whether a column provokes any letters to the Editor. The more the merrier. This, though, took the idea of lively debate to a whole new level. The discussions were going on everywhere. On the internet every news site had some sort of debate going, several with instant polling which invariably registered over 80 per cent in favour of Nigel Hastilow. Friends, for days afterwards, were telling me of unprompted conversations they had with people who volunteered that: "Nigel Hastilow was right". Newspaper letters pages filled with mainly supportive comments. The feature writers got in on the act.

Inevitably, my old paper, "The Birmingham Post," came out against me. "Powell was wrong then, Hastilow is wrong now" its front page leader declared. The politically-correct editor bumbled on about multi-culturalism as if that was the issue. The cartoonist, Bert Hackett, seized the chance to do what he'd always wanted to do and dashed off a caricature of me. I was tempted to write a brief note to the paper which, had I sent it, would have read: "Your front page article demonstrates that 'The Birmingham Post' is out of touch with its readers and goes a long way towards explaining the paper's terrible circulation figures." I didn't do it, though, because it may have been seen as unnecessarily catty. I didn't even retaliate when a columnist on "The Post" blatantly and outrageously libelled me. His attack was bizarre, personal and misinformed. I have never met him nor do I wish to. Had I been the editor of "The Post" I would have been ashamed to carry something so plainly malevolent. I decided it was not worth seeking redress because the paper is now so rarely read and so widely disregarded that drawing attention to it would be playing it at its own desperate game.

This vile vitriol was more than made up for by feature writers in other papers. Simon Heffer in "The Daily Telegraph" was one of my most notable defenders. "The Thunderer" column in "The Times" was another offering support. Rod Liddle in "The Spectator" wrote what was without doubt the clearest and most telling article of the lot. He made clear that the only sin had been to use the words "Enoch" and "Powell" in the same sentence. He found the over-reaction laughable. I had been more circumspect than David Cameron himself, according to Liddle.

Elsewhere opinions varied, as they always do, according to the agenda of the writer. On BBC "Question Time", most of the panellists came out against me. Only one supported me. The audience was evenly divided. The coverage petered out as the week went on but I did make Radio 4's "News Quiz" and TV's "Have I Got News For You?" I am not exactly proud of this but it did demonstrate the resonance this story possessed.

Anyway, I was too busy dealing with another turn of events. Among all the e-mails, phone calls and text messages I was getting were several from leading lights in the Halesowen and Rowley Regis constituency association saying they would not accept my resignation and threatening to take up arms against Conservative Party HQ because they wanted me to stay on as their candidate.

In their eyes, I had done nothing wrong. In the eyes of their friends and families, and more importantly, in the eyes of their voters, it was a scandal that I'd been forced to quit. All I was doing was repeating what everybody thinks. Wasn't it a politician's job to represent the views of his constituents?

When you become a parliamentary candidate, you enter into the life of your constituency and, in particular, the lives of the leading lights in your local constituency association. They become colleagues and friends. You share a common purpose and vision. I had only been in Halesowen and Rowley Regis for six months but that was long enough to establish the beginnings of some good relationships. I felt close to several people and inevitably one or two of them were not at all happy about what had happened to me. They were my friends and sympathised. They agreed with what I had said and saw no reason to apologise for it. And they resented the interference in their own affairs of the central office of the party.

One or two of my friends there were talking about making life difficult for the party hierarchy. There were dark mutterings that they may refuse to accept my resignation. After all, they said, it was they, not the party headquarters, which appointed me and it was they, not HQ, which would decide if I should quit. I had not written to the local party. I wrote to the party chairman, Caroline Spelman.

The risk of rebellion was clear the day after I resigned. That was the reason Caroline Spelman rang me in the morning. She said it was to see if I was all right. Her call can only be described as a fishing trip. She wanted to know what I knew about any potential revolt. I said I'd spoken to several members of the party in the constituency and had heard some wild talk but I was definitely not behind any planned revolt. She reminded me that I had behaved very honourably and hinted that maybe the party might have some other sort of work available for someone with my journalistic skills.

The obvious implication of this was that I should guide the constituency association away from any threat of rebellion. I made no commitment either way. I did not feel I owed the party anything more reassuring than a promise that I was not pushing any such moves.

A few hours later Caroline sent me an e-mail saying David Cameron wanted a word. I replied saying I didn't think anything would be gained by his phoning me. I didn't say I might be very rude to him but that was what I was thinking. After all, he had not deigned to speak to me once in all the time I had been one of his candidates and now, after I had been forced out of the job, he apparently wanted a chin-wag.

If Cameron wanted a word there had to be an ulterior motive. And, of course, there was. He, like his party chairman, wanted to head off a revolt in the constituency and he clearly believed not only that I could take a hint but that I would go out of my way to oblige him even though he had just forced me to quit. That's why I did not want to speak to him.

Driving home that evening down a country lane near Wootton Wawen in Warwickshire, my mobile phone rang (as it had been doing all day). There was no caller identification and I should have not answered it, especially as I wasn't hands-free. But I did.

"Hello Nigel, David Cameron."

I told him to wait while I parked the car by the side of the road. He made a feeble joke about the Immigration Minister Liam Byrne (also, at the time, "Minister for the West Midlands") who had just been fined for driving while using a mobile phone even though it was Byrne who had pushed through the legislation. I wasn't in the mood to laugh.

Cameron told me how honourably I had behaved. He said he was grateful that I had come out with words of support. I had no idea what to say. I was, or at least tried to be, frosty. I did not wish to be rude but I had no idea why Cameron should want to speak to me. Cameron told me that if I needed a shoulder to cry on there were plenty of nice people at the Conservative Party headquarters that I could turn to. I didn't actually reply: "Yeah, right" but I might just as well have done. Rather like Caroline, had told me there would still be work for me to do to further the interests of the party.

Then he asked me how my constituency association was. I said he'd better ask them. How was I to know? I was no longer the candidate for Halesowen and Rowley Regis. Cameron said Andrew Mackay, his parliamentary gofer, would be visiting the constituency to meet the members. Obviously he was trying to encourage me to calm down my constituency association and stop them sticking two fingers up to the party. They were afraid the local Tories would declare the issues Nigel Hastilow raised were too important to become a sacking offence.

It's not that surprising Cameron and Caroline Spelman were worried. Since the weekend, Conservatives in the constituency had been shocked by the level of support the voters were giving to the statement that Britain could no longer cope with uncontrolled immigration. By the Tuesday night, Tory canvassers in one of the Halesowen and Rowley Regis wards had leaflets thrown back in their faces by people who were angry at the way the party had unceremoniously dumped their Parliamentary candidate. It led to a flurry of e-mails in which everyone agreed the party should not have chucked me out and the association was not happy.

Andrew never made it to Halesowen to meet the members. The implication was that he would read them the Riot Act. That wasn't needed because in the meantime various other weapons had been deployed. Shireen Ritchie, Guy Ritchie's stepmother, Madonna's step-mother-in-law, and a Central Office big-wig, launched a charm offensive. She was Mrs Nice while a senior local employee of the party was Mr Nasty. He was ordered to spell out in grizzly detail what would happen in the event of a revolt. The association would be treated like a failing school and put on "special measures". No money, no autonomy, no support. Councillors would find their jobs under threat. They would have the book thrown at them.

So that's why, in the end and despite some brave talk, the Halesowen and Rowley Regis Conservative Association, had no option but to accept my departure and adopt a new candidate.

Yet there was still some further manoeuvring over whether I could reach a compromise deal and find my way back inside the fold. Friends of friends of people in influential positions made "hint-hint" phone calls. They came to nothing. It was difficult to tell how sincere any of it was anyway.

I was left to read through all my e-mails and reflect on the lessons learned from this episode.

Whatever happened to freedom of speech? The question keeps cropping up in the hundreds of the e-mails I received. To the Great British Voter, I struck a chord by saying the unsayable. This was an extraordinary position to be in. All I did was express in plain English what I believed the vast majority of people now think, which is that we must call a halt to unlimited immigration.

When I resigned, the e-mails came in thick and fast. There were too many to count and far too many for me to reply to in person. But when you're under siege it's very heartening to find you still have friends. A few – very few – were rude, insulting or gloating. The vast majority **were** expressions of support and encouragement. They came not just from the Black Country or Britain but from Italy, Dubai, America, Cyprus, Australia – all over the world. Some told personal stories about the lives and concerns of the writers.

My correspondents said how disappointed they were with Britain today. Some said that was why they emigrated; others said that was why they were about to emigrate. An ex-colleague I hadn't spoken to for several years was one such. He had been contemplating a move to France. After what happened to me, he said he was now definitely going.

This is a terrible state of affairs. These people are not right-wing nutters or racist loonies. They are ordinary men and women who are exhausted and exasperated by the way their views are ignored, their opinions are not articulated, their hopes and fears are disregarded. And many of them ask what has happened to free speech. Of course we don't have the freedom to say whatever we wish – various laws limit our ability to say just whatever we want.

But there are more insidious ways of curtailing free speech than invoking the full fury of the law. They include intimidation and fear. It is not racist to say this country cannot cope with more and more immigration. Yet the risk of being branded a racist is so great it is career suicide to say so. My own experience makes that obvious. I am no racist. And while the media have not quite branded me one (for fear of the libel laws, I expect) they have come as close as makes no difference. And plenty of websites have messages describing me as racist. It is not a pleasant situation to be in. Actually, it's terrible.

It is frightening, intimidating and wearing to find yourself singled out for vilification for expressing in public views you know full well most people express in private every day of the week. Because this is what happens, we don't need laws to keep us in line. Fear and intimidation do that for us. That is how political correctness works. Mine is an extreme example. Yet it applies in many areas of our lives. Some of what goes on around us is so patently absurd it makes us scream inwardly. But any public expression of that disgust puts our lives and livelihoods at risk so it's best to keep schtum. Lie low, put up with it and say nothing. It's just easier that way.

When I was up for selection as a Conservative candidate in Halesowen and Rowley Regis, I said I would always express my opinions even if they didn't accord exactly with party policy. I said I believed in the importance of freedom of speech even within the apparent confines of a political party. I also said – and would still maintain – that one of the reasons why most people are cynical about politics these days is because politicians are seen as slippery, insincere, equivocating and only in it for what they can get. My argument was that a candidate who spoke his mind would be welcomed by the voters as a rare commodity. It is clear that I was right. The e-mails and calls I received, the internet polls and news-paper reactions all overwhelmingly proved the case.

On the day I resigned, Caroline Spelman said the tough stance on immigration taken by Michael Howard at the 2005 General Election was one of the main reasons the Conservative Party did so badly. I said I doubted if that were true. She said the party had plenty of private polling evidence to prove it was. That is why the Conservative Party pussyfoots around the issue and dare not address its consequences robustly. It has convinced itself that immigration is a vote loser. Peter Hitchens in the "Mail on Sunday" castigated me for raising an issue which might have won me election at which point I would have failed to deliver any real change in the country's more or less open-door policy because the Tories were no more committed to immigration control than Labour. He was probably right.

The party is terrified of upsetting the politically-correct, left-wing, me-dia-led metropolitan intelligentsia. The people who work for the BBC and "The Observer" are far more important for the Cameron Conserva-tives than the hopes and fears of real people in the real towns and cities scattered across the country they hope one day to govern.

There is something bizarre, as my correspondents make clear, about the fact that even a political pigmy like me is not allowed to raise one of the most pressing issues of our time without being vilified and hounded out.

Admittedly the constraints on freedom of speech are greater than I realised. They include the deliberate twisting and downright nastiness of the political process itself exemplified by the egregious Peter Hain. There's also the fact that a political party can't win if its members are not all rowing in the same direction and I was, apparently, rowing the wrong way.

But above all, we as a nation, are now subject to the tyranny of constant self-censorship to protect ourselves from the wrath of the PC police. That's why I am clearly incapable of being a successful politician but, much more importantly, it's why politicians dare not risk saying what they believe in.

As one of my correspondents reminded me, a song by The Clash summed it all up pretty well: "You have the right to free speech, unless you are dumb enough to actually try it."

The voice of the people

For days after my resignation, the e-mails, and then the letters, came in thick and fast. It was incredibly heartening to receive them because for a while I felt as if I had become a marked man, isolated, a pariah who had broken all the laws of delicacy and decency. I felt as if I were hated or despised and as if I had committed some terrible crime. But every time I began to feel particularly low, I would check my e-mails and so many expressions of support would come tumbling out that they would cheer me up, reassure me and keep me going. Here are just a reasonably random cross-section of those messages (I have omitted the senders' names and details because these were private and they would not have expected their names to be used in public):

"I know we've not always seen eye to eye politically, but I have to say on that on this subject I have more than a modicum of sympathy with your sentiments. My grandfather and grandmother lived in Washwood Heath (Birmingham) when I was a child, doing their shopping in Alum Rock. After a recent visit to the area I was horrified to discover that it was like visiting another country. There is not one white face in Alum Rock or the surrounding area. My grandparents would turn in their graves. The vast majority of the women are covered in veils. Police roam in pairs every 100 yards up and down the High Street, and while I was there several arrests were made involving scuffles with police. Throughout this go-betweens were negotiating with local elders to explain why the police were arresting the individuals. Why? The local indigenous population have presumably been forced to live elsewhere. My mother is terminally ill with cancer. She has had to make numerous visits to the City Hospital in the early days.We have had her transferred purely because she felt intimidated and uncomfortable as if she were visiting a hospital in New Delhi or Afghanistan or somewhere – no friendly faces of her own culture at all to speak of. What on earth have we done? Easy for me to say but stick to your guns. On this one I'm with you completely. I'm all for integration but this is takeover. Huge areas are losing their cultural identity."

"You are unfortunately quite right. I am 64 and since I was young this country has changed utterly and for the worse. We are over-populated in the extreme. Entire communities which survived for generations have been destroyed – what was British and best has gone. We now have yardie gangs, turf wars between drug dealers, Islamic extremists, honour killings, forced marriages and cities that will resemble a foreign country in a few years time, we already have no-go areas where British people feel they can no longer live. Religious schools are brainwashing centres for the next Islamic jihadists – I have been told that one day I and my family will be Muslim by Muslims themselves – they are happy to tell you that they will take over the world but obviously not anyone in authority. Schools should be for education – home and Churches etc for religion. It is nice that we can go and live in other countries now but apart from retired people seeking a better climate most Britons leaving are going because they no longer feel at home in their own country – but then it is not really ours any more. And as for free speech! Gone. My own son has heard people speaking of a civil war in the future as they feel protest is futile. I have friends who emigrated to this country years ago and even they are concerned for their adopted country. I think you were extremely honest about the situation but you will not be heard because the powers that be are either going la la la – or resign when anyone dares to speak the truth."

"Is it time to form a new political party representing traditional conservative values, leaving David Cameron to join the LibDems?"

"'Enoch was Right', this is probably the most repeated phrase in pubs, shops, workplaces etc throughout Britain. I was fortunate to meet and correspond with the man himself, and hear him speak on many occasions. I left the Tory party the day he did. You have done nothing wrong as far as the man in the street is concerned, only stood up for what Enoch called their 'fears and expectations'."

"I do not know you and have never met you, but felt compelled to send you this email expressing my deepest sympathy at your utterly unwarranted, but totally predictable fate. As a politician, you are expected to convey the thoughts of the general public, and raise genuine concerns. There are no greater concerns in this country at the present time, than immigration. Unfortunately, we live in a society that is all too aware of this, but is scared to death of mentioning it in public. There must be millions of people, who at least privately, applaud what you have had the guts to do. Yes, you will of course be labelled as a racist Tory bigot by sections of the limp, liberal, left wing press, but I just wanted to let you know that it takes courage to steadfastly stand up for what you believe in, even in the face of adversity. And to graciously bow out shows that you are an honourable man too. Interesting that no senior figures within the Conservative party have condemned what you have said. Their focus seems only to be on the way your remarks 'could have been taken offensively on this sensitive issue'."

"I am not a political expert, I am a forty-two-year-old Welsh housewife who believes that if we had more MPs like you our country wouldn't be in the bloody state it is today. I recently returned home from Ireland but wished I'd gone to live somewhere else. The immigration scandal means that the British way of life is being eroded for the indigenous population. I am not a racist, neither are you; we are common sense people that can see what the do-gooders are too blind to see in fear of offending the minorities. I sympathise with what you are going through and after reading all the blogs on the internet I can assure you that what you have said is supported by anyone with half a brain. Stand by your comment and make some more. In the meantime, I wish you all the best and salute you for having the guts to state the obvious to people who no doubt would be extremely p***ed off if they couldn't get a doctor's appointment owing to the huge queue of Eastern Europeans waiting to be seen."

"Having tried to obtain a copy of what you actually said yesterday about immigration (as opposed to what others are saying you said about it –I have been in politics long enough to have learned are not necessarily the same thing), so far I have failed to spot anything that you have said that is in anyway inflammatory (whatever 'inflammatory' is supposed to mean - another 'Guardianista' concept, I suspect). No doubt the leadership of our Party can debate ad infinitum whether you should have used other words or phrases in preference to the ones you did; or whether it was 'wise' to even broach the subject at all. However, I for one am grateful that you have. I suspect most of my electors feel the same. It's just make one weep that, as with Patrick Mercer, the party leadership has seen fit make fools of us again by publicly slapping the legs of a candidate who has sought to offer a sincere (and in no way inflammatory) contribution to a debate of crucial importance. I am so sorry that you have felt that you have had no choice except to tender your resignation by refusing, on principle, to accept such an indignity. However, I know the whole constituency party will salute your courage for standing firm. The supreme irony is that, given that even Labour ministers now realise what a terrible genie they have let out of the bottle (and are every day making exculpatory suggestions that we need to 'manage immigration' and 'foster Britishness'), I suspect by this time next year what you have said will seem unremarkable even to the Guardianistas' who have throughout tried to set the terms of reference when talking about race and immigration. However, let me close with some more sage words from Comrade Hodge, who when defending her own immigration faux pas, was at pains to remind us that 'I have spent my whole life fighting for equality... so it is hurtful when people say I am using the language of the BNP, when really what I am talking about is part of the battle against racism'. I think I know you well enough by now to sense that you too would concur with her heartfelt cry. Worshipping myself in a church whose congregation boasts every shade of skin colour there is, and counting amongst my dearest friends refugees and migrant workers from Chile, Lithuania, Philippines, Ethiopia, Sudan, Nigeria and Zimbabwe (to say nothing of my 'I-was-born-here-mate' chums of Afro-Caribbean and Asian descent) I know I certainly would. But, what the heck. We're just 'the racist underbelly of the Tory Party'."

"I and 120,000 other UK people have a house or live in Cyprus, another 59,000 UK people live in North Cyprus. This is because we are fed up with the way the UK is run and that it is no longer our country. The silent majority is right behind you. I am old enough to remember the Enoch Powell speech. My father at the time applauded Enoch Powell but said that nothing would happen until it was too late. My family three generations ago came from Germany and settled down in London. They adopted the UK way of life and worked within the community as silversmiths ... so my family were immigrants. We knew that when in Rome do as the Romans. Speak up Mr Hastilow before it's too late. Look at other countries like Australia; they know how to run things. No job? Get back home. No benefits for 10 years. Don't come into the country, get a week's work so that the National Insurance number can be obtained and then ditch the job and claim. They know all the tricks. Please give us back our country. On Remembrance Day I shall be at The Garrison Church in Dhekalia, Cyprus, with the British troops and I shall remember what a great country we had and the troops who protect us."

"Congratulations to Mr Hastilow for speaking about what is on every English working man's mind. We live in fear of the racist brand when all we are concerned about is the future for us and our children. Well done for speaking the truth."

"I live in Halesowen. I come from a line of traditional Labour Party supporters, but I would like to say you've got my vote in the next election(s). I also work for a large multi national company where positive discrimination is rife. What a change, a politician conveying exactly what his constituents' concerns are. A person cannot question immigration without being labelled racist and this is wrong. The only party that benefits from pushing this issue under the carpet are the vile BNP. Political Correctness will be the downfall of this country!"

"I was both surprised and pleased to hear that a political candidate had the courage to make a statement that reflected his views and more importantly were the views held by of many of his constituents. It has always seemed to me a great pity that the political system in Great Britain has resulted in local people's opinions being ignored in favour of the official party line by aspiring politicians. How refreshing to hear a politician who can look at reality without spectacles tinted either blue or red, and actually listens and represents the views of his electors."

"I am a Tory Councillor and you are right to highlight the dangers of mass immigration. Every year I do a residents survey and immigration is top of the national list of resident's priorities. Many ordinary people agree with your comments."

"It was truly wonderful to hear at long last a public figure expressing the thoughts of many individuals who are not racist but are angered and frustrated at the preferential treatment dished out to those not from our land and the lack of support given to our own."

"The sooner Mr Cameron realises it and publicly reacts to it in a positive way and supports you he will then get the support of many apathetic voters who are sick of the state of affairs here and leaving or want to leave this country."

"I have just read that Mr. Hastilow may be 'sacked'. Why? This country is now a travesty of what it once was. We seem to bend over backwards to accommodate foreigners (who, by the way, don't really want to integrate into our society) but ignore our own people. I am not racist by any means, but this small island, cannot sustain the millions forecast to be here in 20 years' time. We must stop immigration now. Australia has the right idea, why can't we do the same?"

"Immigration is the single greatest concern, the single most talked about issue, of everyone to whom I speak. We need and would vote for a party who would be prepared to stand up and fight politically for the rights of the silent majority who are resentful, angry, afraid, and at present, seemingly voiceless, in Parliament."

"Thank you for saying what most of our thinking. Stand your ground. If they sack you because of speaking the truth, then tell them the Conservatives will never ever get my vote ever again. And I think that would probably go for the rest of the country. Enoch Powell was just ahead of his time."

"Having been under the political spotlight over the weekend I doubt if you would be expecting a message of understanding and support from a lifelong (63 years) supporter of the Labour Party but here it is. In my view Enoch Powell was one of the most brilliant politicians of the 20th Century but sadly will be remembered for something that he wasn't! Despite the popular view, stimulated mainly by the actions of your party, Enoch was not a racist. He was certainly a pragmatist. Fortunately so far there have been no rivers of blood and maybe Enoch's language was a little too strong at the time but the subject of his speech was excessive immigration and it was not racially motivated. The sensitivity at the time arose from the fact that most of the immigrants coming to the UK were from Asia and had brown faces. They were, therefore, easy to identify. To the indigenous Brit (whatever that maybe given our very mixed racial history) a bus load of Polish workers would hardly stand out! I understand that you have only expressed the views of the people you have met on your doorstep canvasses but I can fully understand them. It appears that as members of the EU we have thrown our doors open to fellow EU members without due regard for the socio-economic consequences of the ensuing flood of immigrants. This really is a vast subject. Peter Hain said this morning on Andrew Marr's programme that we are bringing in skilled immigrant workers to fill important vacancies for brain surgeons, teachers, doctors etc. What planet is he on? I know of a number of employers here in South Wales who are filling their factories with immigrant workers almost certainly on below minimum wage levels and in so doing displacing British residents from work and consigning them to the benefit queues. I am afraid that as a nation we are seen as the soft touch around the World. Foreign nationals are allowed to flood in contributing to a population growth that we surely cannot sustain. Then we have a small number of business people who are selling their commercial souls to China but with massive consequential problems. British jobs again being undermined and we are seen to be supporting a Chinese economy that has no respect for environmental matters. I fear that through the nervous fears of David Cameron your own political career might well have been blighted – hopefully not, as the electorate needs politicians that will tell it as it is but if the worst comes to the worst there is always journalism."

"Drive into Thamesmead in south London and see the large Somalian gangs that are causing so much terror. Drive down the Old Kent Road and have a look at the large amounts of Nigerian mini-cab drivers driving battered old cars that are not taxed or insured. Go to Bristol or Nottingham and speak with the locals of all nationalities and ask them what they think. The Mayor of Southall made a statement and asked the question: "Why have we got 25,000 Somalians in this borough?" and the powers that be called him a racialist. Add to all this the strain on the resources in our housing, schools and hospitals with no sign of this mass immigration of these economic migrants slowing down, then it will be a recipe for disaster. What politicians seem to forget and are not taking into account is that these immigrants are breeding faster than the white population."

"I hope you stand your ground and tell your interrogators that you were merely expressing the view – as per your raison d'etre, perhaps – of many of your constituents. I want a representative who tells the country what I think – not what his party bosses suggest I ought to think. What price free speech?"

"Once again when somebody points at the elephant in the room (ie Nigel) and says out loud "Look there is and elephant over there and we must do something about it" - the zoo keepers get annoyed and demand apologies and an admission that we can see no elephants."

"You only said what most of us have been saying for 39 years. We in our household vote Conservative but how they wanted to gag you is disgusting."

"You are completely right to comment that many people say that Enoch Powell was correct in his views. I have heard such statements many times myself - often by people who feel they dare not express such sentiments openly for fear of being branded a racist. You appear to be the victim of a classic case of people shooting the messenger because they do not like the message."

"Unfortunately we are not allowed to say anything that might upset anyone who is not British."

"The Conservative leaders are guilty of stifling freedom of thought and, as a consequence, freedom of expression."

"I regularly read the 'Express and Star' and your column there. Frequently, I disagree with its content! However, having read again the piece published last Friday, I have to say that I could not find anything in that with which I could find fault. This whole business which has led to your resignation seems to me to indicate that you have been the victim of mis-representation and a fabrication of truth. It also seems to me that your Party's leadership, including Caroline Spelman, should have been 'big enough' to see through the media drivel and given you their support and not their 'cold shoulder'. The further revelations in today's edition regarding the requirement that you submit your copy to be 'vetted' before publication is, to me at least, an insult to the high standards of probity and integrity which you have always demonstrated in your published work."

"How brilliant you are to not be brow beaten by political correctness. How right Enoch was and how right you are to tell the truth."

"The bulldog reporter who interviewed you on Radio 5 gave you scant chance to answer the complex question of the connection between blood-shed and mass immigration, and I dare say that in the meantime you have had time to see how the question might best be answered yourself. Nevertheless, here's my feeble effort at an answer, in case it hadn't occurred, or if your head hasn't yet had time to stop spinning. (By the way, I can imagine what you must be going through, and I admire your courage and strength. The greatest source of fortitude, next to faith in God, is a clear conscience in one's own integrity, and thus far you have given every sign of having that.) It seems to me that your example of the 7/7 atrocity is relevant as a dramatic validation of Powell's warning, as was also the violent explosion of tension on Bradford's streets some time ago (and other, smaller "explosions" like the inter-racial violence in the Birmingham suburb last year). The relevance of the 7/7 outrage is that it shows how certain groups of immigrants have brought with them a culture whose fundamental values are inimical to those of the majority of Britons. If left unsupervised, such a culture can then provide a convenient platform for extremists to preach contempt and hatred towards majority values – a hatred which can sometimes be harnessed to commit ideolog-ical mass murder. In short, a cult of death has entered the country along with certain immigrants, leading to one 'successful' and many thwarted massacres. This is only a broad-brush and clumsy attempt at an answer: there is a vast amount more to say – and ask – on the matter, as you so bravely tried to tell the reporter. Moreover, I do not wish that any of this should imply that I endorse the dangerous stupidity of Enoch Powell's style of expression in that infamous yet prophetic speech. You can hardly distance yourself enough from the 'rivers of blood' aallusion. But when I look at the Black Country, I can almost believe that Powell's hysteria was born of the desperation of ever being heard or taken notice of in this perennially overlooked, ignored, taken-for-granted and despised region, which was even then the sink-hole of unwanted people. Thank you for daring to speak up for them."

"Nigel committed a huge crime in today's Britain - he had the guts to speak the truth. Reinstate Nigel and start asking the British people what they think. Many, like myself, are not racist, but are using common sense, and know the immigration issue must be faced head on. To really win votes, follow Italy, and introduce a law to deport criminal immigrants! What an incentive to the others to behave that would provide!"

"Once the truth is 'unacceptable' democracy is at real risk."

"The Tories may not be behind you – but the British public undoubtedly are. You are like a breath of fresh air in a country in danger of being suffocated."

"When someone like you who tells it how it is stands up and gets shot down I think it's a bloody disgrace. The thing is Nigel I believe that all the politicians are thinking what you are thinking and feel the same way. But the bottom line is they value their job salary than standing up like you and saying what the vast majority of people in this country think. After all this is a democratic state and free speech is alive and well if you conform and make it politically correct if they say so."

"I don't hate anyone, I just don't happen to think that immigration is in my interests or the interests of my young children and I don't think that makes me a bad person. What has gone wrong with our democracy when you as a prospective representative of the people cannot voice the honest and heartfelt opinion of the people you are looking to represent? "

"It is a blind man that cannot see the concerns of the British people at this tme. You were brave enough to attempt to bring it to the table. Abu Hamsa was allowed to preach his twisted sermons for years on the streets of this country, David Cameron doesn't have the guts to even let his party talk openly. Shame on him."

"Enoch Powell was right. You only have to walk through any major city or town to realise that Britain is turning into an enlarged U.N. and is ceasing to look like Britain at all. If honest debate is stifled in the way it has over your article and if the truth is not allowed to be heard, the future for our once great country is bleak."

"I am sorry you have had to resign for being the messenger for so many people. At least you did not sacrifice your integrity by refusing to apologise for repeating what many of your constituency told you."

"I'm fed up with being told 'you can't say that'. Intelligent people have been brainwashed over the years by the PC brigade to not see things as they really are. You are that little boy in the crowd who dared to speak out about the Emperors new clothes. Don't give in so easily - the tide is turning. Good Luck."

"Thank goodness some of you are man enough to speak out and say what the nation are actually thinking. It may not be PC to mention Enoch Powell (and there's another issue in itself) but it just beggars belief as to where the current government have actually had their head stuck this last few years as ordinary people are struggling and getting sick to death of what I believe to be the biggest problem in the UK today."

"You are right about immigration; the media and your Conservative colleagues who have criticised your remarks are the ones who should be ashamed. All the leading political parties seem unable to drum up the courage to have an intelligent debate about immigration and as soon as it is mentioned they either hide behind or wave the 'racist' card like frightened rabbits."

"If the London bombings weren't 'Rivers of Blood' what were they?"

"I would just like to express my thanks to you for being one of the few politicians who is ready to stand up and express the thoughts and feelings of a good majority of the citizens of this country. It's heartening to know there are still some trustworthy politicians about, but yet completely disheartening to know that you become the subject of a 'witch hunt' for expressing how people in this country really feel."

"What you said was spot on and is what 75 per cent of the population in this country are saying. Of course to have the guts to speak the truth in this country carries the risk of being accused of being racist, BNP, National Front etc etc. However until people do speak up, as you have done, then we are doomed as a nation. "

"I work (as a part time civilian communications operator in the Police control room) for the xxxx Constabulary. This force, as I'm sure all others are, is riddled with political correctness. We have to go along with it as they are our paymasters but they cannot change the way we think. Anyway, Enoch Powell's words have come to be true. Good luck in your career. If the politically correct do-gooders get their way you will get nowhere. I would be happy for you to be my local MP."

"As soon as I heard the story breaking this morning you became my hero."

"I watched with interest the news relating to yourself and I thought two things. One, I agree with you 150% and secondly, it appears we now live in a country so similar to Communism (no right to speak) that it makes you wonder just where it is all going to end. There is not enough housing for those who originate from here, the NHS on personal experience for the first time recently is about to fold up and is lethal, the police cannot control the crime and the schools are turning out people who don't have a cats chance in hell of getting anywhere. Having driven through South Africa in the Drakensburgs earlier this year I was witness to thousands of school children from 4 to 18 coming out of school at the end of the day. No running water, no electricity, no Mother driven taxis to run them home, all walking for miles but every single one immaculate in dress at the end of a school day. Here in the UK they come out looking like a real heap. You are absolutely right. You can say more in a newspaper than you can as an MP. We haven't lost an MP but gained a spokesperson to represent all those who fear for their country."